NE THE LESS

...TO HIS CHILDREN, GOD NEVER GIVES LESS THAN HIMSELF

By

John A. Knox

xulon PRESS

Copyright © 2003 by John A. Knox

Never the Less
by John A. Knox

Printed in the United States of America

ISBN 1-594670-43-9

All rights reserved. No part of this publication may be reproduced or transmitted in any form or by any means without written permission of the author.

Unless otherwise indicated, Bible quotations are taken from The New Scofield Reference Bible, authorized King James Version, Copyright © 1967 by Oxford University Press, Inc.

Xulon Press
www.XulonPress.com

Xulon Press books are available in bookstores everywhere, and on the Web at www.XulonPress.com.

TABLE OF CONTENTS

Nevertheless	9
Promises Near	11
Offended in Christ	13
Iniquity Visited	15
Iniquity Subdued	17
Why Did God Save You?	19
Who is it That is Really Holding On?	21
Jericho: A Problem or a Promise?	25
Hearing Your Answer	29
What are Your Expectations of God?	31
What Does God Expect from You?	35
On the Basis of Destiny, Not History	41
God Never Loses Anything that Belongs to Him	43
Convictions	47
How Many Whiskers make a Beard?	51
To Covet	55
Need	59
In the Race of Life You're Going to Have Some Pit Stops	61
Chosen Adversaries	65
At Wits' End	67
When Things Aren't Looking Up, You Should	69
His Footstool	73
In Defense of the Unfamiliar	77
Dealing with the Dilemma of Doubt	79
Contemplating the Favor of God	83
Activity	85

Rest in the Lord	87
The Faith of Jesus	91
In Likeness of Lizards	93
Winning	99
In Lieu of Prominence	103
Accounting for God's Generosity	109
Grace and Truth	113
An Ought to Mentality	115
Your Doing Versus Your Being	117
But What About Obedience?	119
A Believer's Obedience and Disobedience	121
The Wrong Time for Grace	123
The Problem of Promises Performed	125
On Being a Witness	127
How to Access Grace	129
You Can't Drive Your Car to Nassau	131
Handling Disgrace with Grace	135
Wounded Oysters and Divine Deliverance	137
Fallen from Grace	139
Bonfires and Burned Out Believers	141
Learning to Lean	145
A Pleasing Walk	147
From His Lips to Yours	151
Great Grace	155
Finding Grace in God's Graffiti	159
Finding Grace in the Eyes of the Lord	165
Sharing the Same Opinion Without Condemnation	167
God's Will and Our Options	169
Sonship Gone Sour	171
The Ever Changing Method of a Never Changing God	173
Himself Alone	177

"Grace is a provision for men who are so fallen that they cannot lift the axe of justice, so corrupt that they cannot change their own natures, so averse to God that they cannot turn to Him, so blind that they cannot see Him, so deaf that they cannot hear Him, and so dead that He Himself must open their graves and lift them into resurrection".

G.S. Bishop

NEVERTHELESS

Psalms 106:8- "<u>Nevertheless</u>, He saved them..."

Much like our Biblical predecessors, we are frequently tempted to settle for less than God's best. To that notion, the Lord would say, "<u>Never the less</u>." Faced with the Red Sea and Pharaoh's charging chariots, the Israelites would have returned to Egypt... the less. The ten spies of Joshua's day would have settled for wilderness land...the less. Jonah resisted Nineveh and chose Tarshish...the less.

Many believe that their failure, their wickedness, their lack of devotion and diligence, and their neglect in remembering the works of the Lord, will serve as the basis upon which the Lord relates to them. Psalms 106:6-10 tells us, "We have sinned with our fathers, we have committed iniquity, we have done wickedly. Our fathers understood not thy wonders in Egypt; they remembered not the multitude of thy mercies, but provoked Him at the sea, even at the Red Sea. <u>Nevertheless</u>, He saved them for His name's sake, that He might make His mighty power to be known."

<u>Never the less</u>!

What would "the less" be? The lesser thing would have been for the Lord to base the success or failure of His people upon <u>their</u> performance, not His.

"<u>Nevertheless</u>, He saved them for His name's sake..." (v. 8)

<u>Nevertheless</u>, "...He rebuked the Red Sea..." (v. 9)

<u>Nevertheless</u>, "... He led them through the depths..." (v. 9)

<u>Nevertheless</u>, "...He saved them from the hand of him that hated them..."(v.10)

<u>Nevertheless</u>, "...He redeemed them from the hand of the enemy..." (v. 10)

The lesser thing would have been for God to have allowed His people to save themselves for their own glory and self-confidence...have His people find their own way through the wilderness...reward His people based upon those who gave the best effort, were the most sincere, diligent, or faithful.

We scoff at this notion, yet many believers embrace the "less", believing it is God when it is not.

It was said of God's people in Psalms 106, that they "...served their idols..." (v. 36); "...sacrificed their sons and daughters unto devils..." (v.37); "...shed innocent blood, even the blood of their sons and daughters..." (v.38), "...were defiled with their own works, and played the harlot..." (v.40). "<u>Nevertheless</u>, He regarded their affliction, when He heard their cry; and <u>He remembered for them His covenant</u>..."(v. 44-45).

The <u>Lord</u> remembered <u>His</u> covenant. Their actions and attitudes did not invalidate His covenant. Since God's people didn't make covenant with Him, they could not break covenant with Him.

How do you measure the greatness of God's mercy?

How do you fathom the vastness of God's grace?

You begin measuring the magnitude of God's grace by the magnitude of man's sin. His grace is greater!

For the Lord to give His people what we deserve is to give us "the less." To place our destiny in our own hands is "the less." A significant portion of our declarations to the Lord should be the cry, "<u>Never the less</u>!"

From Heaven's throneroom the Lord God is saying, "<u>Nevertheless</u> I will save you for my name's sake, that I might make my mighty power known." This declaration reveals the One who deserves <u>all</u> glory and praise.

PROMISES NEAR

☗

"Thou art near, O Lord..." (Psalms 119:151). "I do set my bow in the cloud, and it shall be for a token of a covenant between me and the earth" (Genesis 9:13).

It was a beautiful spring day...not a cloud to be seen. The persistent glow of a brilliant sunshine made moisture a necessity for the recently planted flowers. As water filled the garden hose and rushed past the partially thumb-covered opening, a fine mist of life-sustaining liquid filled the air and gently settled over the thirsty blooms. Each flower seemed to awaken, as if to say, "thank you".

Contrary to what you would expect on a sun-drenched morning, a perfect rainbow suddenly appeared in the mist filled air above the flowers. Each burst of moisture served to expose the ever-present color filled spectacle.

What never would have been expected was proven to be ever near, awaiting only the proper moment and situation to be revealed.

As God set a rainbow in the clouds for Noah as a perpetual testimony of His covenant, likewise, each promise from Him to you is always near, awaiting the proper moment and situation to be revealed.

Believers often fall prey to an "out of sight, out of mind" way of thinking. We readily embrace things seen, while believing less in promises unseen. The Lord not only has His eye upon us, He sees

His promises near us continually. Knowing that in the midst of trouble we often forget his unseen covenant with us, our Father has retained for Himself the total responsibility of remembering His covenant for us. He told Noah, I will remember my covenant, which is between me and you..." (Genesis 9:15a). His word to us is the same. "And He remembered for them His covenant..." (Psalms 106:45a),

Though unseen, incubating until the moment needed, every promise the Lord has ever made to you is always near. The validity of each promise is not dependent upon you seeing or remembering His covenant. He has reserved that responsibility for Himself! The consistent nearness of His promises is assured by the constant nearness of His presence.

OFFENDED IN CHRIST

Matthew 11:6 "And blessed is he, whosoever shall not be offended <u>in</u> me".

There is a great difference between being offended <u>by</u> Jesus and being offended <u>in</u> Jesus. Many are offended by Jesus. He was a great offence to the religious Pharisees and Sadducees of His day. The words He spoke and the life He lived defied their rules and regulations. Jesus was to them, as to all unbelievers, "...a stumbling stone and rock of offence" (Romans 9:33). "For they stumbled at the stumbling stone" (Romans 9:32).

It is reasonable that unbelievers be offended <u>by</u> Christ Jesus. His declaration of Lordship and His supernatural life stands as an ongoing contradiction to any life that attempts to reach God or please God by human effort. Ultimately the life of Jesus invalidates, rendering null and void, every act of human endeavor.

As a child of God you are found "<u>in</u> Jesus". Every troubling situation and adverse circumstance must pass through Him before it can touch you. Each individual that may be the instrument of such testing, is carefully selected for the task. This is the providence of God.

In the midst of trial, testing and great trouble, every believer will either be blessed or offended, but either way, it will be "<u>in</u> Christ".

To be offended <u>in</u> Christ is to believe that Jesus should do what He could do on your behalf instead of what He is doing. In a moment of great distress you will be reminded that He could deliver you immediately and spare you all the suffering. Yet He often chooses not to do so. To be blessed is to recognize that what He is doing at the moment is always secondary to that which He has already done at the cross. For it was at the cross that we were placed "<u>in</u> Christ". To be "<u>in</u> Christ" is evidence enough that you have passed from death unto life and are no longer subject to those things that in times past offended you.

The blessing of being "<u>in</u> Christ" is that you can be offended, but you don't have to be. Praise is the evidence you're not.

INIQUITY VISITED

"...The Lord, The Lord God merciful and gracious, longsuffering and abundant in goodness and truth. Keeping mercy for thousands, forgiving iniquity and transgression and sin, and that will by no means clear the guilty, visiting the iniquity of the fathers upon the children and upon the children's children unto the third and fourth generation" (Exodus 34:6-7). "For the Lord is good; His mercy is everlasting; and His truth endureth to all generations" (Psalms 100:5).

The exposing of our sin and failure is something we expend great effort to avoid. There is significant Biblical precedent for such activity. After their sin, Genesis 3:8 says "...Adam and his wife hid themselves from the presence of the Lord". King David had an intricate plan to dispose of Uriah and make Bathsheba his wife. He even allowed her the expected time of mourning (2 Sam 11:27) to help insure that his iniquity would remain hidden.

In spite of our vain attempts to cover our sin, the greatest confirmation that you have found grace in God's sight is that He visits your iniquity. In your humanity, you cannot imagine a worse predicament. As a child of the King of Kings, you can have no greater confirmation of His love for you. The magnitude of your sin is important only because it serves to demonstrate the greater grace that eradicates your failure.

Moses desired desperately to know God's ways. In Exodus 33:13 Moses says to the Lord, "…if I have found grace in thy sight, show me now thy way, that I may know thee, that I may find grace in thy sight…And He said, My presence shall go with thee, and I will give thee rest" (Exodus 33:14). Rest from the onslaught of sin and iniquity can only be found in the presence of the Lord. Unless he visits your iniquity, you will have no rest from it. Though David said "…my sin is ever before me…" (Psalms 51:3), he rested in the God Who could cleanse him "…whiter than snow…" (51:7), create in him "a clean heart…" (51:10), make him "to hear joy and gladness" (51:8), restore unto Him "…the joy of Thy salvation; and uphold…" him (51:12), and cause David to say, "O Lord, open Thou my lips; and my mouth shall shew forth Thy praise" (51:15).

All men will be found by Him. All their iniquity will be visited. For everyone that concludes that their own goodness is adequate, they will be found condemned by guilt. Mercy doesn't clear the guilty until it is received. For those who believe that the goodness of the Lord is their only hope, they will be found redeemed by grace.

Visiting your iniquity is not only God's preference, it is His way for us to know Him, and thus, find grace in His sight. He desires to be gracious to you, and show forth His mercy. The guilty, who have no sense of need for God's grace and mercy, will remain guilty. But His mercy is so vast, so immeasurable, that He holds in reserve enough to be everlasting to all generations. He covenants to visit the father's iniquity that has passed down upon all following generations for all of time. And as He visits and passes before His people, <u>He proclaims</u> this: "The Lord, The Lord God, merciful, and gracious, longsuffering, and abundant in goodness and truth, keeping mercy for thousands, forgiving iniquity and transgression and sin…" (Exodus 34:6-7).

As He visits your iniquity, rejoice! It is His way of bringing redemption.

INIQUITY SUBDUED

"He will turn again; He will have compassion upon us; He will subdue our iniquities; and thou wilt cast all their sins into the depths of the sea" (Micah 7:19).

Iniquity will not be harnessed or constrained by your efforts to do so. It is so well disguised as religious activity and good works, that unless God extends compassion and mercy, discerning otherwise would be impossible.

Your iniquities begin under your control, then get out of control, and remain so, until God brings them under His control. He subdues them because they are so vast only He can do so. He also subdues them because He is merciful! How does God subdue our iniquities? How does He relate to us in the depths of our wickedness? His Word says, "...when I sit in darkness, the Lord shall be a light unto me" (Micah 7:8). "...He shall bring me forth to the light, and I shall behold His righteousness" (verse 9). "Who is a God like unto thee, who pardoneth iniquity, and passeth by the transgression of the remnant of his heritage? He retaineth not his anger forever, because he delighteth in mercy" (verse 18).

God subdues our iniquities with His righteousness. Your righteousness will not do. His righteousness manifested is Jesus! All of your iniquity was placed upon Jesus at the cross. Jesus was "...bruised for our iniquities..." (Isaiah 53:5).

So complete was the work of the cross that the writer of Hebrews 10:16-17 declares, "This is the covenant that I will make with them after those days, saith the Lord; I will put My laws into their hearts, and in their minds will I write them, and their sins and iniquities will I remember no more."

By <u>His</u> righteousness despair has become deliverance, disgrace has become delight, and remorse has become redemption.

WHY DID GOD SAVE YOU?

"...He delivered me, because He delights in me" (Psalms 18:19).

A favorite part of Sunday night and Wednesday night church service was testimony time. Wonderful stories were told about <u>how</u> one was saved. Often a sharing saint described <u>when</u> and <u>where</u> he got saved. Despite the encouragement and inspiration that came to the congregation as a result of these declarations of faith and gratitude, I do not recall ever hearing a testimony concerning <u>why</u> someone was saved.

What would motivate a Holy God to redeem you? Is there anything about us that would cause the Lord to draw you and I unto Himself? Perhaps the best way to answer the question, "Why did God save you?" is to understand the reasons why He didn't save you.

God did not save you because of your great <u>decision making</u> abilities. You did not choose God. He chose you! "But ye are a chosen generation..." (I Peter 2:9), (see I Corinthians 1:26-29). The twelve disciples were so because they were chosen (Luke 6:13), not because they chose Jesus. Even Saul, a man with an aptitude and proficiency for making correct religious decisions, could not choose Jesus. Jesus said in Acts 9:15, "...Go thy way, for (Saul) is a chosen vessel unto Me, to bear My name...". In John 15:6 Jesus said "Ye have not chosen me, but I have chosen you...".

You were not saved because of your ability <u>to do</u> for God. To insist on co-redeeming ourselves would insure our damnation. Our redemption is solely based on the Lord's performance (Ephesians 2:8-9; Philippians 1:6).

Your <u>decency</u> cannot serve as the reason God saved you. If this were true, the first expression of indecency would nullify your hope for eternal life. Believing that man's righteousness is no more than "...filthy rags..." (Isaiah 64:6) makes any claim to decency deluded and foolish.

<u>Distinctiveness</u> cannot be the reason God saved you. When Christ is removed from your life, there then is absolutely no difference, or distinctiveness, between you and the vilest of sinners. (see Romans 3:19,20,23). Your good effort, good works, good looks, or good attitude does not make you distinctive. Jesus does.

Perhaps you <u>deserve</u> salvation. Romans 6:33 says that "the wages of sin is death...". Death, destitution, and destruction is what you deserve.

So, why did God save you? Why did He freely give His Son, who knew no sin, to become sin for you, that you might be made the righteousness of God Himself? God saved you because He <u>delights</u> in you! That's right! God delights in you! Believe it. It is true. Psalms 18:19 tells us that "...He delivered me because He delighted in me..." Isaiah 62:3-5 reveals God's heart, saying, "...as a bridegroom rejoiceth over the bride, so shall thy God rejoice over thee." Zephaniah 3:17 describes your Father's incredible love for you when it says, "The Lord, thy God, in the midst of thee is mighty; He will save you, He will rejoice over thee with joy; He will rest in His love, He will joy over thee with singing".

The fact that God saved you because He delights in you is startling evidence as to the extent and comprehensiveness of God's love. His love is far broader and deeper than any sin ever committed. Scripture reminds us "...for love shall cover the multitude of sins" (I Peter 4:8). No sin is left uncovered. "And their sins and iniquities will I remember no more," saith the Lord (Hebrews 10:17). What a delight! What a relief!

WHO IS IT THAT IS REALLY HOLDING ON?

๛

"The eternal God is thy refuge, and underneath are the everlasting arms…" (Deuteronomy 33:27)

In the midst of your greatest storms you will be told to "just hold on to God". Every ounce of your strength and endurance will be tested, but do not let go of God. "Holding On" is an assignment God has never given you!

God has a better plan…Himself! He said, " Fear thou not; for I am with thee. Be not dismayed; for I am thy God. I will strengthen thee; I will help thee; yea, I will uphold thee with the right hand of my righteousness" (Isaiah 41:10). The right hand of Father God is Jesus. Your Father holds you "in Christ".

In recent years the following story has been widely published and is of great encouragement.

> Some years ago on a hot summer day in south Florida a little boy decided to go for a swim in the old swimming hole behind his house. In a hurry to dive into the cool water, he ran out the back door, leaving behind shoes, socks, and shirt as he went.
>
> He flew into the water, not realizing that as he swam toward the middle of the lake, an alligator was

swimming toward the shore. In the house, his mother, while looking out the window, saw the two as they got closer together. In utter fear, she ran toward the water, yelling to her son as loudly as she could.

Hearing her voice, the little boy became alarmed and made a U-turn to swim to his mother. It was too late. Just as he reached her, the alligator reached him.

From the dock, the mother grabbed her little boy by the arms just as the alligator snatched his legs. That began an incredible tug-of-war between the two. The alligator was much stronger than the mother, but the mother was much too passionate to let go. A farmer happened to drive by, heard her screams, raced from his truck, took aim and shot the alligator.

Remarkably, after weeks and weeks in the hospital, the little boy survived. His legs were extremely scarred by the vicious attack of the animal. And on his arms were deep scratches where his mother's finger-nails dug into his flesh in her effort to hang on to the son she loved.

The newspaper reporter, who interviewed the boy after the trauma, asked if he would show him his scars. The boy lifted his pantlegs. And then, with obvious pride, he said to the reporter, "But look at my arms. I have great scars on my arms, too. I have them because my Mom wouldn't let go".

If the outcome had depended upon the child's efforts to hang onto the mother, the child would have perished. Life in Christ does not depend upon how well you hang onto Jesus. You can be certain that your eternal destiny solely depends on Jesus, the strong right arm of the Father, never letting go of you.

On your journey there are many opportunities to be scarred. You will often rush past the warning signs and wade into dangerous waters. You will be scarred by terrible choices. You will ignore Godly counsel and set out on missions where failure is certain, and consequences are painful. But you will never journey beyond God's love and care.

Some of your scars will be marks of a loving Father Who holds you tightly in His grasp. His imprint will be upon you as a reminder of His faithfulness, not yours. Rejoice. For the hands of Jesus that hold you bear the scars from His Father Who would not let Him go…nor you "in Him".

JERICHO:
A PROBLEM OR A PROMISE?

"And the Lord said unto Joshua, see, I have <u>given</u> into thine hand Jericho, and its King, and the mighty men of valor" (Joshua 6:2).

The Israelites were exactly where the Lord wanted them to be. They were walking by faith in the promised land. While moving at God's direction they were confronted with a large obstacle, a difficulty, a problem of great magnitude. Jericho stood between them and where the Lord wanted them next on their journey.

In Joshua 5:13-15 we find Joshua surveying the topography around Jericho. He was looking at his problem. He was devising a strategy for overcoming and conquering. He was developing a theology for triumph.

At this moment, what is it that you see as your greatest difficulty? What obstacle stands between you and victory? What is your problem? What is your Jericho? Whatever you see, or consider to be, your greatest difficulty, God does not see it as so. God's "...thoughts are not your thoughts... His ways are higher than your ways, and his thoughts are higher than your thoughts" (Isaiah 55:8-9). Whatever you consider to be your greatest problem, God says it is not.

Your dilemma is, that when faced with great difficulty, you try to deal with the "Jericho problem" before you deal with the "Jesus problem". Dealing second-handed with Jesus is our greatest problem. Jericho wasn't a <u>problem.</u> Jericho was actually a <u>promise.</u>

In Joshua 3:13 Jesus appears to Joshua for the purpose of reminding Joshua that Joshua's focus was to be on Jesus, not Jericho. Jesus appeared as Captain of the host to confirm that the battle, the difficulty, the obstacle was already destined to be conquered. But the conquering would occur as a promise of God, and not according to the plan or performance of Joshua. Joshua clearly heard his marching orders as given by the Captain of the host. His response to Jesus is recorded as part of Joshua 5:15:"And Joshua did so." Joshua has now dealt with Jesus. He has dealt with his greatest obstacle. Jesus is Joshua's sole priority. Jesus is now in His rightful place.

Joshua 6:1 says, "<u>Now</u> Jericho"…(Now…not too fast. Now…not any sooner. Now…Jericho). Jesus says, "See, I have <u>given</u> into thy hand Jericho…" (Joshua 6:2). Jericho is not a problem at all. Never has been. Jericho is not a problem because it, too, is in its rightful place.

God says to you, " I know you got up this morning with your "Jericho" on your mind. But "Jericho" is not your priority. I AM!" Did you get up this morning thinking that finances were your problem? Did you conclude that a physical need was your greatest difficulty? Did you presume that your marriage relationship, in-law relationship, or some other troubled relationship was your problem? Are you attempting to deal with your Jericho before you deal with Jesus? Why? Jesus has <u>already</u> dealt with your Jericho. But you will never fully receive the gift of your Jericho until you deal with Jesus. His <u>doing</u> begins at the point of your <u>undoing</u>.

The overcoming of your Jericho is the promised result of dealing with Jesus. It is His gift to you. You have been made "<u>more than conquerors through Him</u> that loved us…" (Romans 8:37); "For whatever is born of God <u>overcometh</u> the world; and this is the victory that <u>overcometh</u> the world, even our faith. Who is he that overcometh the world, but he that believeth that Jesus is the Son of God?"(I John 5:4-5). These verses are reality because the battle, the obstacle, the problem is not yours; it is the Lord's (2 Chronicles 20:15).

Do not presume you will know how God does His work. He is the never changing God with the ever changing method. But remember,

His method is not the focus. His timing is not the focus. Even the end result is not the focus. He, and He alone, is the priority.

"By faith the walls of Jericho fell down..." (Hebrews 11:30a). <u>Deal with the Problem-solver, and what you thought was your problem will be revealed as a promise to be received.</u>

HEARING YOUR ANSWER

♕

"In the beginning was the Word, and the Word was with God, and the Word was God" (John 1:1).

Regarding Joseph, Psalms 105:19 says, "Until the time that his (Joseph's) word came; the word of the Lord tested him." While you wait on your word from the Lord, with what Word is God testing you? Joseph was in a dilemma. He had been given a dream…a word from God, but from where he stood it looked meaningless. Yet he was receiving the "word of the Lord" for everyone else but himself.

The chief butler had a dream that generated many questions. In Genesis 40:12-13, Joseph had God's word for the chief butler. The chief baker also had a dream that produced questions for which the baker had no answer. In Genesis 40:18-19, God's word came to Joseph as the answer to the chief baker. Yet two years later Joseph still remains in prison with no word from God in answer to his own petitions. Why was he in prison? Was this God's reward for integrity and loyalty? If imprisonment is the favor of Almighty God at work, would he have been better off without His favor? If prison is necessary, was thirteen years of it necessary? Had he been forgotton?

Joseph was being tested by the "word of the Lord". One of the great testings of life comes when you know the answer to another's question, while God's answer to your own inquiries remains hidden.

A friend is overcome with anger, and the root of bitterness is glaring to you. A loved one struggles, and you can clearly detect the deeper workings of God in the arenas of patience and self-control. The primary preoccupation of your acquaintances are their questions. To you, their answers are easy, and conspicuous. Yet you wonder at God's reluctance to respond to your anguished cries...

Joseph's quandary continues in Genesis 41:1-8 as Pharaoh's dream created confusion for which no magician or wise man had answers. Again, God's word for Pharaoh was revealed to Joseph...

Suddenly, at the precise moment of God's choosing; at the decisive, well defined, sovereignly ordained instant, the Lord Himself hastily delivered Joseph out of his dilemma (Genesis 41:14). Joseph saw the fulfillment of the God given dreams. Joseph's word came.

Perhaps we could paraphrase Psalm 105:19 to read, "Until the time that your "word" comes; the Word of the Lord will test <u>you</u>". It is so easy to look to the dream, the vision, the word as the place your destiny is found. Jesus, the Word, is also the Way, and it is in Him that you must journey. The fulfillment of "the word" given you is not the destination. Jesus is. He will not share His throne with any "word"...even when He gives it. So He takes you through circumstances that dethrone the "word" so that the Living Word will be your chief desire.

WHAT ARE YOUR EXPECTATIONS OF GOD?

"But this man, after He had offered one sacrifice for sins forever, sat down on the right hand of God, from henceforth <u>expecting</u> till His enemies be made His footstool" (Hebrews 10:12-13).

What are your expectations of God? What is it that He can do for you? What have you been waiting for Him to do for you...for your family? How many years has it been since you first petitioned Him for an answer to that critical issue? For many, the time for high expectations, undeterred hope, and enduring faith has long since expired.

The limit of your doing, your thinking, your being, is the beginning of the ability of God. In order to fully experience and encounter the ableness of the Father, at least two events must occur. He must first bring you to the end of yourself. <u>Your</u> expectancy will certainly perish. <u>Your</u> hope will die. <u>Your</u> faith will become extinct. This process is the fulfillment of Galatians 2:20, "I am crucified with Christ ...I live, yet not I, but Christ..." No longer will you be able to rededicate yourself, but only renounce yourself.

Encountering Christ will annihilate <u>your</u> hope, <u>your</u> faith, and <u>your</u> expectations. There will be a moment when you will be convinced that no longer can you expect Abba Father to move on your behalf. You will be tempted to believe that those long dark nights on your knees were lost upon your Father who was dealing with matters of the more expectant and faithful of His children. You will be wrong.

Your decrease births His <u>increase</u> in you. Your demise makes way for His fullness. As He removes you, He gives you Himself.

Jesus has expectations of the Father. <u>Jesus has expectations of the Father for you.</u> When you find yourself at the end of your hope, Jesus is your hope. He is the hope by which you draw near unto your Father (Hebrews 7:19). You have no other hope. He is the "...hope set before us, which hope we have as an anchor of the soul, both sure and stedfast, and which entereth into that within the veil" (Hebrews 6:18-19).

When you are at the end of your faith you are called to rest in the faith <u>of</u> Jesus ("...and the life which I now live... I live by the faith <u>of</u> the Son of God"...(Galatians 2:20), and His reliance on the Father. He has an expectation of the Father on your behalf. The reason God is doing above and beyond what you can ask or think is because He is responding to what <u>Jesus asks and thinks of Him on your behalf</u>. Can you imagine the extraordinary things God will do in response to the expectations of Jesus for you? No longer do you stand in your own confidence of Father God. You actually stand in <u>Jesus'</u> confidence of the Father.

Shadrach, Meshach, and Abednego declared that, "...our God... is able to deliver us..." (Daniel 3:17). Paul convincingly proclaimed, "...for I know in whom I have believed and am persuaded that He is able..." (2 Timothy 1:12). Daniel's victory in the lion's den was the answer to King Darius' question, "...O Daniel, servant of the living God, is thy God...able to deliver thee from the lions?" (Daniel 6:20) To the Ephesians Paul declares, "Now unto Him who is able to do exceeding abundantly above all that we ask or think..." (Ephesians 3:20).

Regarding the issues of life that you have persistently held before the Lord in prayer, Jesus has higher expectations of your Father. Not only does He "...ever liveth to make intercession for them..." (Hebrews 7:25), But, "for as the heavens are higher than the earth, so are my ways higher than your ways, and my thoughts higher than your thoughts" (Isaiah 55:9). Jesus simply knows the great and mighty things to expect of the Father, on your behalf. The highest calling is for you to live in <u>His</u> expectation of the Father, not yours.

WHAT DOES GOD EXPECT FROM YOU?

"Being confident of this very thing, that he who hath begun a good work in you will perform it until the day of Jesus Christ" (Philippians 1:6).

What does God expect of you? Does He expect you to be obedient, holy, dedicated, faithful, loyal, and committed? What do you expect from yourself? What are your expectations of others?

In your desire to please the Father, you will most often relate to Him on the basis of what you believe His expectations of you are. If God the Father is your coach, how well you perform will determine how pleased you think He is with you. If God the Father is your judge, how you keep the rules and regulations will determine whether or not you're meeting His expectations. If God the Father is your friend, you will work hard to be a good friend. Many Christians believe that God's expectations of them are so lofty and elevated that the Lord will never really be pleased.

What is the basis and source of your expectations? The scripture tells us that our expectations should come from God. Psalms 62:5 says, "My soul, wait thou only upon God; for my expectation is from Him." What you can always expect from Him is <u>Him</u>. Expect no less from Him than Himself. As you begin to expect Himself in every circumstance, the reality of what God expects from you is brought into sharp contrast. He expects only your death. Jesus instructs us in John 12:24 that until a seed dies, it cannot bring forth life and fruit. As a believer, the wicked man has perished. You are a new species, a new creation (2 Corinthians 5:17). Let your expectations go. Do not hold on to them. Let them die. Let them perish. You will be delightfully surprised how God redefines what He expects of you, and what you can expect of Him and others.

Be warned that you cannot die at your own choosing. If permitted, you will always choose to survive. You will defend yourself. You will gather others about you for the purpose of your vindication. But die you must if you are to meet God's expectations.

If you cannot choose your own death, who will see to it? God will do what you cannot do. The Lord Himself will oversee your death. He will do so for Christ's sake. How else could Jesus meet His Father's expectation? How could Jesus resurrect and give life to you without your death? There is no resurrection without a death. God expects you to die. It is His pre-requisite for living.

Your Father is so committed to this process that He will use every means and everyone at His disposal to produce the desired outcome. Do not be surprised when He chooses to use your closest friends and loved ones as instruments in the procedure that He is overseeing. For they are, most often, the ones in which we have placed our greatest expectations.

The Lord does not expect you to be obedient, holy, faithful, or loyal. In fact, He knows already that you cannot do those things. Jesus met every expectation of the Father, including the Father's expectations of you. You now can "...be confident of this very thing, that He who hath begun a good work in you will perform it until the day of Jesus Christ..." (Philippians 1:6). You will be delighted to know that "Faithful is He that calleth you, who also will do it" (I Thessalonians 5:24).

<u>God's expectations of you are met, not because you are faithful, but because Jesus is faithful on your behalf to the will of the Father. The Lord's expectations of you are not based on your loyalty or commitment to Him. They are met because of His unconditional commitment to you.</u>

This revelation will free you from your expectations of others. As we relate to people we see them through the Father's eyes. We see their failure and weakness as avenues through which His grace and power flow.

<u>Grace always releases you from your expectations into God's expectations.</u> <u>Grace does the same for your "brother".</u>

As a believer, I can be wrong all day long and still be righteous. The persistent urge to be right, correct, or at least vindicated, is self-righteousness.

ON THE BASIS OF DESTINY, NOT HISTORY

"But as it is written, eye hath not seen, nor ear heard, neither have entered into the heart of man, the things which God hath prepared for them that love Him" (I Corinthians 2:9).

Jesus became your history through His death, so that you might live out your destiny through His resurrection. Jesus precedes our past and exceeds our future. He is eternal.

When you became a new creature in Christ Jesus (2 Corinthians 5:17), you became a new being...a new species, with a destiny that Jesus secured, and a history that He forgave.

Moses was born into slavery in Egypt under Pharoah's rule (Genesis 1:11-13). He was born under a curse of death (Genesis 1:22). So were you. Even though one event that catapulted him toward his ultimate destiny was murder (Genesis 2:11-13), and even though he responded to confrontation with fear (v. 14), and fled (v.15), God's destiny for Moses was not determined by Moses history. Moses' destiny was determined by God! As you recall, Moses was not in the desert searching to find God. God went to the desert to find Moses. Even when the Lord told Moses what his specific destiny was as God's instrument of deliverance, Moses wanted no part of it. God was not deterred.

As Gideon threshed wheat and hid fearfully from the Midianites, "...the angel of the Lord appeared unto him, and said unto him, the Lord is with thee, thou mighty man of valour" (Judges 6:12). The Lord had just announced Gideon's destiny.

Gideon was so deeply immersed in his own history, that he could not believe the word of the Lord regarding his own destiny. As Gideon informed the Lord that in his family history he was the least of the least, God was saying to Gideon, "...thou shalt smite the Midianities as one man" (Judges 6:16).

The Saul of history became Paul of destiny.

The Jacob of history became Israel of destiny.

The same Judah who committed adultery with Tamar, his daughter-in-law, was destined to become the tribe of Judah that gave us Jesus.

Rahab of history was the harlot of Jericho. Rahab of destiny is in the lineage of Jesus (Matthew 1).

His plans for you far exceed your most grandeous thoughts. The magnitude of God's vision for you is beyond human imagination. Your destiny is the ongoing resurrection power and life of Christ. Your destiny is not limited to what you see or sense. It is all that God sees and declares to be true concerning you.

The Lord has not allowed your destiny to be dependent on you. As His child, He has reserved that privilege for HIMSELF! Be at rest. His thoughts about you far exceed your own. In Jesus, you have the assurance of both a history forgiven, and a destiny beyond your wildest dreams.

GOD NEVER LOSES ANYTHING THAT BELONGS TO HIM

"And Israel said, It is enough; Joseph my son is yet alive; I will go and see Him before I die" (Genesis 45:28).

You remember the moment, though obscured by heartache. A small child's simple declaration, "I want to ask Jesus into my heart", is one of just a few pieces of evidence upon which you hold tightly. Any fruit of that transforming event has been overwhelmed by the helplessness of watching your child, your son or daughter, decline, then descend into the depths of sin and destruction. Your hope is on life support. As months become years, you question whether memories once cherished are only wishful thinking.

For thirty years Jacob believed that his son, Joseph, was dead. After selling Joseph into slavery, his brothers took his coat of many colors, killed a goat, and dipped the coat in the blood. Recognizing the coat as Joseph's, and believing he had been killed by a wild animal, Jacob said, "…It is my son's coat; an evil beast hath devoured him; Joseph is without doubt torn in pieces" (Genesis 37:33).

All of the facts before Jacob pointed to his son's demise…the coat…the blood…the witnesses…the disappearance. Each passing day, month, and year became the body of evidence needed to confirm Jacob's worst fears.

Yet God had never lost sight of Joseph. At every turn, the Lord's eye was upon him. The pit could not hide Joseph. Slavery could not. Prison could not. "But the Lord was with Joseph, and showed him mercy, and gave him favor in the sight of the keeper of the prison" (Genesis 39:21). Joseph was forgotten in prison by the chief butler, but not by God.

In Matthew 18:12-13 Jesus said, "How think ye? If a man have an hundred sheep, and one of them be gone astray, doth he not leave the ninety and nine, and goeth into the mountains, and seeketh that which is gone astray? And if so be that he find it, verily I say unto you, he rejoiceth more over that sheep than over the ninety and nine which went not astray".

The parable of the lost sheep has been used often as an effective and enduring message of redemption and evangelism. Please note though that it is a story of a lost <u>SHEEP</u>, not goat. The lost sheep belongs to the shepherd. The shepherd pursues the lost sheep because the lost sheep belongs to him. The man has "…an hundred sheep…" (verse 12). He is not chasing after a stranger's sheep. In the parable, the shepherd seeks the one who has strayed. There is no evidence that the sheep is looking for his shepherd. Never does the shepherd say, "I have ninety nine obedient well-behaved sheep that give me little trouble, therefore, I will not be bothered by this one sheep who is so troublesome".

You may be tempted to make a declaration similar to Jacob, and say, "An evil beast has devoured my son, he is without a doubt torn in pieces". Your confidence dropped off the radar screen years ago. Your hope turned into despair. Your expectancy became despondency. The body of evidence you see and sense is all that is needed to confirm you worst fears. BUT GOD NEVER LOSES ANYTHING THAT BELONGS TO HIM!

He does not misplace His sheep. His sheep do not stray because the shepherd is negligent or disinterested. Every lost sheep is a divine opportunity for Father God to express His unconditional love. It is His occasion to save them,"…for his name's sake, that he might make his mighty power to be known" (Psalms 106:8). It is the juncture in the journey where the gift of repentance is embraced, forgiveness is received, and restoration is evident. The greater the need, greater is the measure of grace. The greater the grace, greater is the glory to behold. The greater the glory, the more the Father Himself is revealed! Hallelujah.

CONVICTIONS

"Peter answered and said unto him, though all men shall be offended because of thee, yet will I never be offended" (Matthew 26:33).

Has God called you to be a man or woman of strong convictions? Every individual has convictions, strong opinions, definite positions, and confident judgments about specific issues and activities. As a young attorney, I regularly encountered thieves who thought nothing of burglarizing a home or business, but had a strong conviction against robbing a person by using force. I routinely interviewed those who would steal, but never from the elderly or infirmed. Many have convictions about lawbreaking, unless the laws broken involve going over the speed limit, or "borrowing" office supplies from an employer.

Christians with strong convictions give occasion for hypocrisy. Having a vigorous conviction against murder and manslaughter, the sins of gossip and slander produce very little remorse or repentance. While standing in staunch opposition to the holocaust of World War II, the church remains substantially immobilized in the dark shadow of abortion.

God has issued no call upon your life to be a person of conviction. Your convictions are the evidence that you have taken sides on a certain issue for the moment. A conviction is a position of your choosing. It is nothing more. Is it any wonder that the strong opinions and persuasions of many Christians is the very tool that Satan uses as a wedge to separate believers from one another? How often do you have a conviction about something that God has no conviction about at all? Convictions are admirable, but not Biblical.

You have been called to be a person of <u>faith</u>, not a person of <u>conviction</u>. Faith in Whom? Jesus; none other. Noah never attached one piece of gopher wood upon the Ark because it was his <u>conviction</u> to do so. Noah prepared the Ark "By <u>faith</u>..." (Hebrews 11:7), and thus ...became heir of the righteousness. Abraham never entrusted his son Isaac to God because of a personal conviction to do so. He did so "By <u>faith</u>..." (Hebrews 11:17)

"By <u>faith</u> Moses forsook Egypt ..." (Hebrews 11:27). Egypt is a type, or picture, of the world system, or worldliness. "Choosing rather to suffer affliction with the people of God than to enjoy the pleasures of sin for a season" (Hebrews 11:25), Moses said "No" to Egypt. He did so not as a matter of personal conviction, or resolve, but as a man of <u>faith</u>, by <u>faith</u>. <u>You likewise will overcome the world no other way</u>.

Romans 10:17 says, "So, then, faith cometh by hearing, and hearing by the word of God." There is no faith possible unless God Himself initiates it by speaking a word. How you respond to a word from God is faith. <u>A man of faith then is a man who lives his life in response to what God is saying. A man of conviction lives his life in response to a situation, event, or circumstance.</u>

Convictions are often good, but they are not God. A conviction is not evidence of you having responded to a word from God. <u>Faith is</u>. <u>Faith is God initiated</u>. <u>A conviction is man initiated</u>. As a Christian, your ability to know what is righteous, and the power for you to act in a manner pleasing to God is not accomplished by conviction. Instead, it is a response to the Lord's speaking to you at some time and place along your journey.

The way you live your life should never be decided by what seems right. "There is a way that seemeth right unto a man, but the end thereof are the ways of death" (Proverbs 14:12). Anything that seems right to you as a believer, yet produces alienation, fragmentation, strife, or any other work of death and destruction in the Body of

Christ is merely the fruit of your own conviction. It will not endure the fire that purifies true gold. Faith abideth forever. Faith will endure the fires of time (I Corinthians 13:13). For this reason you are called to be a person of faith, not conviction. There will be a time when even your strongest personal conviction cannot stand the rigors of constant assault. But by faith you will overcome and endure.

The next time you abstain from evil, from temptation, or wrong doing, do so believing that "…it is God who worketh in you both to will and do of His good pleasure" (Philippians 2:13). Understand that forsaking Egypt, (the world) can only be accomplished by faith, not personal conviction (Hebrews 11:27).

To further distance the element of faith from personal conviction, the life of a believer has been so changed, that you now live life not so much by faith in Christ as you do by the faith of Christ Himself (Galatians 2:20; Philippians 3:9). Your life then is no longer a compilation of convictions and principles. <u>Your life is Christ</u>! To Him and Him alone be all glory.

HOW MANY WHISKERS MAKE A BEARD?

"And their sins and iniquities will I remember no more" (Hebrews 10:17).

For many years our family business had a policy forbidding employees from wearing a beard. After selling our business to another firm, the new owners had no such policy. Every employee who had been restrained from growing facial hair in order to comply with the old policy, suddenly started growing a beard. Several men grew attractive, fully developed beards. Many others grew a very unsightly and revolting collection of hairs that made people who looked upon them long for the days of the old policy.

If there is a minimum number of hairs required to comprise an official beard, many employees would have fallen short of the minimum requirements. Their defense to criticisms of their beard-growing attempt could have been to simply deny that they had a beard at all. The quantity of their whiskers surely fell short of the number needed to have officially been bearded. A glance around a crowd of people reminds me that the question, "How many whiskers make a beard?" is still open for debate.

Undebatable though is your need for God's grace. Your need for the grace of God is explained by being reminded of the answer to the question, "How many sins make a sinner?"

Though it takes more than one hair to make a beard, one sin is all that is needed to condemn you for eternity. There is no greater measure of grace needed to save a murderer or molester of children than to save a liar or one pridefully boastful. "For all have sinned, and come short of the glory of God..."(Romans 3:23). It is your sin, whatever it is, that condemns you. "The wages of sin (that which you earn) is death..." (Romans 6:33).

Jesus did not come to save you from hell. He came to save you from sin. How does he do that? "For he hath made Him (Jesus), who knew no sin, to be sin for us, that we might be made the righteousness of God in Him"(II Corinthians 5:21). What an incredible event. What a glorious sacrifice. What a wonderful and loving Lord! Romans 5:19 tells us, "For as by one man's disobedience many were made sinners, so by the obedience of One (Jesus) shall many be made righteous (right with God)."

Jesus was made sin. You were made righteous. The law can only expose sin. It cannot deal mercifully with sin. It cannot rescue you from sin. The law offers no hope for your sin, only condemnation. The law deals with individual sins. Jesus deals with the sin of an individual, once for all.

Jesus never dealt with sin by degree, because there is no degree of sin. There is sin, period. The remedy for your sin had to be greater than the measure of your sin. God triumphed over sin by giving you Jesus. Thus, victory over sin is in Jesus, not the law, because the law is inadequate to deal with it. The law can tell you when you are wrong; but it cannot set you right. Jesus fulfilled the law and thus set you right. The remedy of even the "slightest" sin is Jesus, because even the most minute sin sent Jesus to His death. In light of that fact, there is no trivial sin. There is no slight sin. There is only sin...sin that ultimately necessitated the cross.

Was Jesus really made to be your sin? Yes. The evidence for this was His death. For the wages of your sin was His death. Having dealt with sin instead of winking at it, having paid the cost through the sacrificing of His Son, Christ Jesus, God "...by one offering...hath perfected forever them that are sanctified..." (Hebrews 10:14), and now says, "...I will put my laws into their hearts, and in their minds will I write them, and their sins and iniquities will I remember no more" (Hebrews 10:16b-17).

Much more than merely being "saved by a whisker", your ... "so great salvation ..." (Hebrews 2:3) is the act by which God redeems man for eternity through the shed blood of His Son, Christ Jesus.

TO COVET

Romans 13:9-"...Thou shalt not covet..."

Psalms 24:1 "The earth is the Lord's and the fullness thereof; the world, and they that dwell therein".

To covet is <u>not</u> to want what someone else has in their possession. To covet is failing to recognize that what you possess belongs to God. In other words, coveting begins when you believe what you possess is <u>yours</u>.

Based on that false conclusion, you will conclude next that what someone else possesses is actually theirs. Ultimately, when you believe that what you possess is yours, it will be logical to believe that what someone else has, <u>ought</u> to be yours. Either one is coveting from the Lord God.

Such thinking has brought great turmoil, hurt, and strife into human relationships. It has complicated our existence, and greatly distorted the truth of a <u>sovereign</u> Lord. A deflated perception of God regrettably coincides with an inflated perception of ourselves.

In Psalm 50, the Lord is very clear about ownership. "For every beast of the forest is <u>mine</u>, and the cattle upon a thousand hills. I know all the fowls of the mountains; and the wild beasts of the field are mine. If I were hungry, I would not tell thee; <u>for the world is mine, and all the fullness thereof</u>" (Psalms 50:10-12).

To believe for a minute that you actually own anything is to covet that which is the Lord's and His alone. Even your own life has been purchased, and you are not your own.

Job, who possessed much, lost much, and possessed even more again, seemed to have understood God's ownership when he said, "...The Lord gave, and the Lord hath taken away; blessed be the name of the Lord" (Job 1:21). Acknowledging His ownership sets you free from covetness.

"Our spiritual life is not the struggle of an earnest will and an upright spirit against the power of evil; but it is the all-sufficient strength of the Lord Jesus Himself living in us and overcoming the forces of evil, so that we think and feel and act as Christ would through the power of the Christ that lives within us."

A.B. Simpson
"Life More Abundantly"

NEED

"But my God shall supply all your need according to His riches in glory by Christ Jesus" (Philippians 4:19).

Things you desire and things you need have been perceived to be the same in many instances. They are not. Much of what you desire originates in your heart. That which you need originates in the heart of God. You do not create need...He does.

Need is your friend, not foe...and ally, not adversary. It is a gift. It is God's method of providing to you Himself. Need brings you to the place where the inadequacies of self-reliance are evident... where human supply is quickly exhausted...where only God Himself will satisfy. You will conclude ultimately that your greatest need is Himself!

It is never promised that your desires would be met according to God's riches in glory. Desires can usually be attained by persistent effort and diligence. Those that settle for such reward will experience the satisfaction of having attained their goals and desires. Such satisfaction is temporal, and falls far short of the riches of the glory of God by Christ Jesus.

Need is God's means of providing you Himself. The greatness of your need is one method the Father uses to demonstrate the greatness of your God. His response to your need is to "...supply <u>all</u>

your need according to His riches in glory by Christ Jesus". Need is not optional…it is a necessity if you are to testify as to His riches in glory. Your need becomes the window into heaven where God's riches in glory are not only revealed, but become personalized by Christ Jesus.

Only need can transform this mystery into reality. As God's riches in glory unfold for you, your desires become secondary and your needs are revealed as gifts for which you give God praise.

You soon will welcome need as you would a close friend. You will recognize that need is the track upon which God's abounding grace flows to you.

"Let us, therefore, come boldly unto the throne of grace, that we may obtain mercy, and find grace to help in time of need" (Hebrews 4:16).

Need is not evidence of God's dissatisfaction with you. To think so is to make yourself the issue. You are not. Your need is evidence of God's satisfaction with <u>Himself</u> as your sole supply! Your need is all about <u>Him</u>!

IN THE RACE OF LIFE, YOU'RE GOING TO HAVE SOME PIT STOPS

"And Benaiah, the son of Jehoiada, the son of a valiant man, of Kabzeel, who had done many deeds, he slew the two sons of Ariel of Moab; he went down also and slew a lion in the middle of a pit in the time of snow" (2 Samuel 23:20).

For Benaiah, this day had begun like any ordinary winter day. The snow rapidly accumulated as the cold wind blew. Having accomplished his mission for the King, Benaiah speedily traveled the familiar road toward home. The pathway he journeyed had become so customary to him that he could traverse it easily, even in the dark of night.

The day could have gone no better. Scripture tells us that Benaiah, the "son of a valiant man, who had done many deeds, slew the two sons of Ariel of Moab..." (2 Samuel 23:20). Soon he would hear the approving voice of King David. As one of David's mighty men, his stock was on the rise. His place in the Kingdom seemed secure. His influence with the King was ever expanding. His father would be proud. The favor of God was no more evident on any man than Benaiah. Then suddenly... "He went down..."

Have you ever noticed how quickly circumstances and situations change? Perhaps this is why the Lord reminds us often that joy results from our lives being Christ-dependent, not circumstance-dependent. If you assume that your hope and joy results from a few good situations, you have only a false hope and fabricated joy, both of which will quickly dissipate should adversity alter the circumstances. Scripture tells us that Benaiah's situation was transformed quickly. His circumstance was altered. "He <u>went down</u> also and slew a lion in the middle of a pit in time of snow" (2 Samuel 23:20). "He went down..." Why is there always a down side to our journey with the Lord? Is the going "down" not escapable? Is it not avoidable? Certainly more diligence, more attentiveness, more commitment should help us avoid falling into the pits. Really? What is "the pit"? It is any place or set of circumstances that you wish you were not in, and you would give almost anything to be free from. You may call it a trial, a test, a trouble, or a tribulation. To Daniel it was a lion's den. To Jonah it was the belly of a fish. To Shadrach, Meshach, and Abednego, it was fire. Even though a pit comes in all shapes and sizes, you will most assuredly know when you are in yours. Not only was Benaiah in a pit, he had an <u>adversary</u> in his pit. His opposition was a lion. Yours is also. "Be sober, be vigilant, because your adversary, the devil, like a roaring lion, walketh about, seeking whom he may devour" (I Peter 5:8). In the pits of life you will find yourself face to face with your adversary. You cannot hide. You cannot run.

Get the picture. Benaiah is in a snow covered pit, facing a hungry lion, with no means of escape except by conquering his adversary. He is not equal to the conflict. The lion seems to have the advantage. Benaiah would not have chosen this fight. So God chose the conflict for him. Benaiah would have selected a more convenient place and time. If you ever must fight a lion, you do not fight him in the snows of winter. A snow cover makes for poor footing. You will slip. You will slide. You might fall. Your hand will be cold, making the grasping of your sword nearly impossible. You will undoubtedly dress for winter, and thus, will be wearing far too much clothing. Your own abilities and agility for fighting will be diminished. Also, a lion is most hungry in the winter. Food is scarce. To have a potential victim fall into your lap, in a time of snow, is every lion's dream. Overcoming the pit is not measured by how "equal-to-the-task" you are. The fact is, you have been made unequal to the task! It is by God's design. It is a design for which you should give Him praise. As the Lord places you in situations that seem impossible and overwhelming, you are best served by concluding quickly that you, in and of yourself, and not equal to the task at hand. This revelation can lead to only one truth...God is able.

History serves us well in recording God's ableness. He is equal to our tasks. From a natural perspective, what was equal about a boy named David and the man Goliath? Were five creek bed stones equal to a sword in the hands of an enraged giant? Pharaoh recognized the inequality of his situation with Moses. The ruler of Egypt had difficulty taking the words of a shepherd seriously. Surely Jehosophat recognized that he was unequal to the task at hand when he dispatched the choir to face the Assyrians in battle. What was equal about Gideon's three hundred men against the battle-ready Midianite army? The disciples quickly concluded that they were unequal to their task of feeding 5,000 men, plus women and children, with five loaves of bread and two fish. Shadrach, Meshach, and Abednego did not know the outcome of the struggle in their pit. Yet their testimony was clear... "...our God ...is able to deliver us..." (Daniel 3:17).

Your pit stop will always be a place where your brilliance, your resources, your intellect, your charisma and charm will fail. You will be unequal to the task. Yet when you have nothing left to rely upon but God, you will discover that in Him you have all you need.

Benaiah's name means "God has built". He was under construction. The process was not finished. Before he could be "built up" into what God had in mind for him to be, Benaiah had to "go down" into the middle of a pit. He had to discover that the God who created him would be the God who sustained him. In due time the lion was slain. I have often wondered if the corpse of Benaiah's adversary became the footstool upon which he stood to escape his pit...

CHOSEN ADVERSARIES

♛

Numbers 13:29- "The Amalekites dwell in the land of the Negev; and the Hittites, and the Jebusites, and the Canaanites dwell by the sea, and by the edge of the Jordan."

The Israelites had God's promise of a land of milk and honey. The nation had both heard and experienced the promises and provisions of their God. He had faithfully fed them, protected them, provided for and led them. As the people drew near to possessing the land of promise, a perplexing problem arose.

Not only was God's word true about the land of milk and honey, but His word was also true that their promise was being occupied by Amalekites, Hittites, Jebusites, Amorites, and Canaanites. Why did God leave enemies in the land? What good is a promise that is permeated with adversaries?

The Lord chooses your adversaries! Their selection is planned, predictable, and purposeful. They are never more than you can bear, but they are more than you can bear alone. God planned it that way. Far greater than His promises of strength, protection, provision, and such, is the marvelous overriding promise of His presence. Your adversaries are the tool the Lord uses to expose two truths: He exposes your weakness, and reveals His almightiness and strength. These two revelations are brought to light in His presence. An adversarial opponent is a small price to pay for such a glorious encounter.

Adversaries are gifts, chosen especially for you. They are prepared and provided by the Father to reveal Himself.

The battles of life are never won by how you respond and relate to your adversary. They are won by how you respond and relate to the word of God. His word usually comes in the form of a promise, with an adversary camped right in the middle of it.

"In everything give thanks, for this is the will of God concerning you…" (I Thess. 5:18). Yes, that's right. Go ahead, Try it. Thank the Lord for your adversaries. They are chosen by God especially for you.

The quicker you see your adversary as His provision, the sooner you will see the Father revealed.

Oh, by the way, the Lord said as regards the Amalekites, Hittites, Jebusites, Amorities and Canaanites, "By little and little **I** will drive them out from before thee, until thou be increased, and inherit the land" (Exodus 23:30).

AT WITS' END

"They reel to and fro, and stagger like a drunken man, and are at their wits' end" (Psalms 107:27).

I have great admiration for any person who can live by their wits. Some folks have a natural ability to fix anything and do just about everything. They listen to a malfunctioning engine and know what to do. A craftsman takes a few tools and supplies and builds a structure of beauty and durability. Long ago I arrived at the conclusion that a person living by his wits could survive almost anything.

I picture Peter as a man who could live by his wits. A fisherman by trade, I am reasonably sure he was handy at many skills. He could live by his wits.

In Matthew 14:22-23, there is a story of a storm that severely tested Peter's wits. He was in a "…boat…" (verse 24). The time was "…in the fourth watch of the night…" (verse 25). The darkest hour was upon Peter and his companions. There was no compass, no direction, no assurances, and no clear vision of what was to be. They were overwhelmed. Life was out of their control. Their wits were useless, unable to preserve them.

At some point Peter either got "scared out of his wits" or merely came "to wits' end." In either case, he discovered that neither his charisma, keeness, ingenuity, talent, intelligence or natural ability could save him. Merely living by his wits was not enough. It never is. So, he got out of the boat to get to Jesus.

<u>Only when you arrive at your wit's end can you go to Jesus</u>. You will never cry unto the Lord in your trouble until He brings you to wits end. <u>He reveals Himself at the end of yourself</u>.

The storm never was the disciples' trouble. Their real dilemma was their self-reliance…their wits. Psalms 107:23-31 says, "They that go down to the sea in ships, that do business in great waters; These see the works of the Lord, and His wonders in the deep. For he commandeth, and raiseth the stormy wind, which lifteth up the waves thereof. They mount up to the heaven, they go down again to the depths: their soul is melted because of trouble. They reel to and fro, and stagger like a drunken man, and are <u>at their wit's end.</u> Then they cry unto the Lord in their trouble, and he bringeth them out of their distresses. He maketh the storm a calm, so that the waves thereof are still. Then are they glad because they are quiet; so he bringeth them unto their desired haven. Oh that men would praise the lord for his goodness, and for his wonderful works to the children of men!"

Our Lord is looking for a person who trembles at His word, not at storms. He is orchestrating the storms of life to bring us to our wits' end. This revelation will not only cause us to rejoice as He disperses the storm, but as He initiates it. Praise Him for what He is doing, and even more for who He is. He is delivering us <u>from</u> our "wits". He is delivering us <u>to</u> Himself.

WHEN THINGS AREN'T LOOKING UP, YOU SHOULD

༺

"And when these things begin to come to pass, then look up, and lift your heads; for your redemption draweth nigh" (Luke 21:28).

We are a people who study our problems. There is no work shortage for those we employ to help us problem solve. Counselors, consultants, advisors, analysts, psychologists, psychiatrists, therapists, negotiators, attorneys, arbitrators, and more, are all actively involved in society's quest to resolve problems. For believers of Christ Jesus, your attention needs to shift from your problems to God's promises.

I suspect that there is no problem in life for which the Lord God has not proclaimed a promise. His promises are all gifts, and gifts can only be possessed (claimed) when they are received. Every trial, every test, every trouble is the occasion to either focus on your problem or give attention to God's promise. God has a promise for every problem. If you doubt this, you have been problem focusing.

The issue is not, "how are you dealing with your difficulty." The issue is, "how are you dealing with the <u>Lord Who</u> is dealing with <u>you</u> in your difficulty."

Judges 6 speaks of troubled times for the nation of Israel. These were evil days (v.1). These were days of disobedience to God (v.10). The Midianites were prevailing against God's people (v.2-6). Oppression had been the rule for seven years. Fear gripped the lives of the Israelites. There was no revival, no renewal movement, no restoration, and no record of repentance.

In the midst of these problems, what were God's specific promises?

Judges 6 depicts a conversation between Gideon and God. In verse 12 the "...angel of the Lord appears unto Gideon, and said unto him, <u>the Lord is with thee, thou mighty man of valor</u>."

Gideon replies in verse 13, "...if the Lord be with us, why then is all this (difficulty) befallen us? And where are all His miracles...?" Gideon continues on, "But now the Lord hath forsaken us..."

But God says in verse 14 to Gideon "...<u>thou shalt save Israel</u>." Gideon seems amazed that his Lord could be so mistaken. He reminds God that his "...family is poor..., and I am the least in my father's house." In other words, I am the least among the least.

But The Lord says, "<u>Surely I will be with thee, and thou shalt smite the Midianites as one man</u>". (verse 16).

Gideon and the Lord seem to be conducting two distinctly different conversations. The Lord was freely offering His promises. Gideon was focusing on his problems. When problem solving becomes your focus, God's promises are easily forgotten. A promise forgotten, dismissed, debated, or doubted is a promise not received. Your problems will cry out for rationale, reasonable solutions. The difficulties in life will demand that you "step-it-up a notch." Our Lord often allows these troublesome times to "take-you-down" a notch in order that His purposes be accomplished in you. After all, "God...giveth grace to the humble" (1 Peter 5:5). In other words, He gives Himself to the humble. The promise of Jesus, the Captain of the Host, is God's answer to your Midianite problem. King Jesus is God's promise to you. The Lord always addresses your problems with His Promise.

In Judges 6:17 Gideon finally raises the real question. He tells God that "If now I have found grace in Thy sight..." Perhaps it is at this moment Gideon realizes that neither the Midianites nor his own low estate are his problems. The issue is, has the Lord promised grace for the occasion? Will Gideon be given the ability to know, and the power to do, the will of the Father God in the situation? Can Gideon now journey joyfully in the expectancy of God's promises, instead of being distracted by the evidence of his own problems?

The greatest struggle is not how to overcome your difficulty. Your greatest challenge is recognizing and receiving God's promises that pertain to your problem. Promises received are problems resolved.

HIS FOOTSTOOL

♛

"Thou preparest a table before me in the presence of mine enemies…" (Psalms 23:5).

Why would the Lord prepare a feast for you in the presence of your enemies? My vision of a glorious celebration includes the presence of friends, not enemies. "…In the presence of enemies" inhibits both a good appetite and digestion. Can you remember a meal with your enemies that was cause for celebration?

In ordering your steps, sovereign God brings you and your enemies together in one place…<u>His presence</u>. His enemies are your enemies…your enemies are His. Every battle fought by His children is in His presence, therefore every enemy is a defeated enemy.

The place of engagement with your enemy is always at His footstool. "For He must reign, till He hath put all enemies under His feet" (I Corinthians 15:25). God's declaration to Jesus is no different. "…sit thou at my right hand until I make thine enemies thy footstool" (Psalms 110:1).

The issue, however, is never your enemies. The issue is always the presence of Father God. The place of defeat for your enemy is simultaneously the place of worship for the believer. "Exalt ye the Lord our God, and worship at His footstool…" (Psalms 99:5). "We will go into His tabernacles; we will worship at His footstool" (Psalms 132:7). As you worship in His presence at His footstool, your adversary, which is also His enemy, is being "made His footstool" (Hebrews 10:13).

Believing this truth will not only cause the return of a good appetite, but even in the presence of your enemies, it will make the celebration one of heavenly proportions.

"He is Peace when we are in the uncertain places of life. He is Power when we are weak. He is Joy when happiness has run away and hidden. He is Hope when circumstances shout it is all over. When we can find no answer, He is the answer. When we have failed, He is our righteousness. When there is no way out, He is the way out. He is our beginning and our end and everything in between. He is our life."

Steve McVey
Grace Walk Ministries

IN DEFENSE OF THE UNFAMILIAR

"So Abram departed, as the Lord had spoken unto him..." (Genesis 12:4).

One of the primary reasons that fear and anxiety are so prevalent in the lives of many Christians is because of our love for the familiar. Familiarity causes our flesh to be confident in itself, confining us to a life of fear of the unfamiliar.

Journeying in <u>unfamiliar</u> places forces us to <u>calculate with God</u>. As life's journey is lived out in response to our Lord's calculations, the journey then becomes the destination. Jesus said "I am the way..." (John 14:6a). He then is both our Journey and our Destination.

Jesus desires to rescue us from the familiar. He sees the familiar things in a believer's life as one of the greatest obstacles to finding God. Security and refuge seem to be the benefits and blessings of familiarity. But it is a false security and an unsound refuge. Lifeless churches are filled with believers who seek the security of the familiar more than the truth of Christ, when only the truth can set them free. The Lord said unto Abraham in Genesis 12:1, "...Get thee out of thy country, and from thy kindred, and from thy father's house, unto a land that I will show thee."

What is the "father's house"? For Abraham it was his family, his country, his upbringing. For you it is something you hold close and dear. The familiar "father's house" is a place of permanence in our life that has caused us to stop on the journey. Maybe it is a tradition, a doctrine, a custom, a belief, a form, or way of doing things. It seems safe. It appears secure and dependable. It is mostly right. It is certainly worth defending. It is a point of reference; a fixed position; a hand-me-down theology from someone you most likely respect, admire, and love. It is something you identify with and from which an important part of your identity comes. It seems so good, so right, but it will keep you in a fixed position, immovable, at a standstill. When God moves on, you will ultimately spend your energy and a valuable portion of life defending something Jesus is not sustaining. "And Moses took the tabernacle, and pitched it outside the camp, afar off from the camp,... and it came to pass that every one who sought the Lord <u>went out unto the tabernacle of the congregation, which was outside the camp</u>"(Exodus 33:7). If you will journey with Jesus, you will do so <u>outside</u> the place of familiarity. He is calling for an end of your calculations. To become familiar with Jesus, "<u>Let us go</u> forth, therefore, <u>unto Him outside the camp</u>, bearing His reproach"(Hebrews 13:13).

Jesus says, "I will never forsake thee" (Hebrews 13:5). As you forsake the familiar, you will hear His voice. Your response to what you hear Him say is the journey.

DEALING WITH THE DILEMMA OF DOUBT

♛

"Then saith he to Thomas, reach here thy finger, and behold my hands; and reach here thy hand, and thrust it into my side; and be not faithless, but believing. And Thomas answered, and said unto him, My Lord and My God" (John 20:27-28).

There comes a time in the life of every believer when one struggles with doubts about God, salvation, heaven, and other eternal matters. For many the struggle brings the validity of their salvation into question.

If you had real faith in God would you ever doubt Him? Could you ever doubt the person and work of Christ if you truly and completely trusted Him? Is persistent doubt a sign that you do not know God the Father at all? Is there a difference between doubt and unbelief?

For you, the believer, Jesus will often offend your mind in order to change your heart. Your mind is most offended when Jesus conducts Himself in a manner contrary to your opinion of what should be, or when Jesus brings about an outcome, or orchestrates a situation, that contradicts your strongly held sentiments.

Doubt, then, facilitates humility. For God to change your heart He must offend your mind. Doubt is a sure sign that God is challenging the conclusions, judgments, and opinions your mind has embraced in lieu of truth. This occurs as God resists your pride and as He teaches you not to be offended by whatever Jesus is doing.

In John 11:1-6 we see John the Baptist struggle with doubt. John is in prison (verse 2) and facing certain death. Jesus is teaching, preaching (verse 1), healing and delivering (verse 5), and apparently drawing some large crowds. John sends two of his disciples to Jesus and instructs them to ask Jesus if Jesus is really the Son of God, or should he still be expecting another (verse 3). John had proclaimed the coming of Jesus. John had preached, "Repent; for the Kingdom of Heaven is at hand" (Matthew 3:2). He was described as "the voice of one crying in the wilderness, prepare ye the way of the Lord...", as prophesied by Isaiah and spoken of in Matthew 3:3. He baptized Jesus (Matthew 3:13). He had seen and fellowshipped with Jesus. Yet now John is in prison. He is to be beheaded. His situation is causing doubt to rise in his mind. Maybe this One called Jesus was not the Savior spoken of by the prophets of old. Perhaps John had been mistaken. Possibly John had misspoken. It would be a fatal blunder to die a martyr's death on behalf of a Savior Who was so busy teaching that He could not deliver John from prison and death.

Jesus' response to John's doubt was to tell John "...blessed is he, whosoever shall not be offended by me" (Matthew 11:6). Blessed is the person who understands that however Jesus is working, He is working for your good. Blessed is the individual that comprehends that when Jesus works contrary to our strongly held sentiments and opinions, and when Jesus brings about an outcome that is in opposition to our expectations, that His work is an act of mercy, because "...mercy covers all His acts."

Jesus never chastises John for his doubt. He does not reprove John for his sudden lack of confidence and trust. Instead, Jesus assures John that He is in control even though the circumstance and outcome seem to indicate otherwise. Jesus offended John's mind in order to change his heart. With no hint of denouncing Jesus, and with no evidence to indicate John mistrusted any further, Scripture later reveals that John died a martyrs death, perhaps again,

"...preparing the way of the Lord...", as Jesus would soon journey the same way.

Unbelief is the rejection of truth. Doubt is the questioning of truth. Jesus condemns unbelief, not doubt. Doubt occurs when the foundation of your faith is called into question. Unbelief exposes the lack of any spiritual foundation.

An unsaved person is only capable of unbelief, not doubt. You can only doubt what you have at one time believed. Thus, to doubt is a sure sign that you are saved. Unbelief is a sure sign that you are not.

Do not be plagued with guilt or condemnation because of doubt. Under God's watch care, doubt is of great benefit. Doubt is never dealt with until you have a personal revelation of Jesus Himself. Thus a believer's doubt is worthwhile, because its only remedy is Jesus Christ revealed.

CONTEMPLATING THE FAVOR OF GOD

※

"For thou, Lord, wilt bless the righteous; with favor wilt thou compass him as with a shield" (Psalms 5:12).

Father God grants favor to His own children. He favors you with Himself. His favor is not only expressed by what He does on your behalf, but far more so, by Who He is on your behalf.

The numerous troubles of Job caused friends and loved ones alike to assume that he had fallen into God's disfavor. To conclude this is to believe the favor of God is judged by the hand of God. It is not! The indicator of the Lord's favor is the heart of God. Despite Job's grief and testings, Job said, "Thou hast granted me life and favor, and Thy care hath preserved my spirit" (Job 10:12). The psalmist has said, "...in His favor is life" (Psalms (30:5). Scripture further exclaims that "...in (the Lord's) favor our strength shall be exalted" (Psalms 89:17).

God our Father is about His business of favoring His children in many practical ways. "Whoso findeth a wife findeth a good thing, and obtaineth favor from the Lord" (Proverbs 18:22). He who finds wisdom "...shall obtain the favor of the Lord" (Proverbs 8:35). "A man right with God obtained favor of the Lord" (Proverbs 12:2). King David was a man..."Who found favor before God..."(Acts 7:46).

Pharaoh has mistakenly been credited with granting favor to Joseph that subsequently resulted in Joseph being made governor over Egypt and the house of Pharaoh. However, Acts 7:9b-10 tells us that "...God was with him (Joseph), and delivered him out of all his afflictions, and gave him favor and wisdom in the sight of Pharaoh..." Joseph's success before Pharaoh was <u>God's favor</u> upon him, not Pharaoh's.

At an earlier time God demonstrated His favor to Joseph while Joseph was in prison. You will note that God's favor did not bring Joseph deliverance <u>from</u> prison, but rather, it brought Joseph deliverance <u>in</u> prison." But the Lord was with Joseph, and showed him mercy, and gave him favor in the sight of the keeper of the prison...because the Lord was with him, and that which he did, the Lord made it to prosper" (Genesis 39:21,23).

When you measure God's favor by His hand, you will be tempted to believe that your predicament or trouble is a sure sign of the Lord's disfavor. To His children, His heart is a heart of compassion and mercy. His heart is a heart to be trusted. His heart overflows with love and favor toward you. The true measure of God's favor is not His hand toward you, but His heart.

ACTIVITY

"The zeal of the Lord of hosts will perform this" (Isaiah 9:7).

Being a Christian has become synonymous with being busy. With days full of activity and obligation, Sunday is seldom a day of rest. Sunday may be a day of worship, congregating, interacting, and worthwhile activity, but for those people taking part in the schedule, it is rarely restful.

What does it mean to rest in the Lord? One fruit of grace at work in your life is rest.

When the Bolshevik revolution occurred in Russia in 1917, the Russian Christian Church was convening in Moscow. Only six blocks away from fierce street fighting in which hundreds were being killed, the Christian church closed its convention with a two-day debate on whether church officials should wear red or yellow robes at church functions. When the convention adjourned, they had neither robes to wear nor churches in which to wear them. Communism had taken over. Bibles were confiscated, churches were burned, ministers and congregations were murdered. "They knew not what was happening until the flood came and swept them all away. That is how it will be when the Son of man comes" (Matthew 24:39).

Resting in the Lord is not slouching, slothfulness, or slumbering.

One who rests in the Lord is one who has "... ceased from his own works..." (Hebrews 4:10). A person who slumbers is an individual whose life fails to produce good works, because he is very busy producing dead works. Dead works is anything you're doing to make you more loved or accepted by God. A slumbering spirit stays busy doing nothing. This does not suggest inactivity, but instead, much activity unanointed and not initiated by God. The aforementioned church in Russia slumbered with activity.

God never anoints activity that He does not initiate. Jesus was very clear in limiting His own activity to the will of the Father. Jesus said in John 6:38, "For I came down from heaven, not to do mine own will but the will of Him that sent me".

There is no call upon <u>you</u> to start something for God. There is no Godly favor upon anything <u>you</u> begin. There is no pressure upon <u>you</u> to accomplish some great eternal thing. From the beginning, <u>He</u> and He alone creates. He sustains. He accomplishes all eternal things.

The work of you matters not. The work in you is eternal. It is so because He is doing it. "Being confident of this very thing, that he who hath begun a good work in you will perform it until the day of Jesus Christ" (Philippians 1:6).

REST IN THE LORD

"...And His rest shall be glorious" (Isaiah 11:10).

There is only one thing that makes your adversity glorious... <u>His</u> rest in the midst of it. Rest is His gift to us, made more likely to be received through trial. "Come unto me, all ye that labor and are heavy laden, and I will give you rest" (Matthew 11:28). HE IS AT REST in your trial.

Your call to rest in the Lord will be challenged most often in the midst of adversity. In the Book of Habakkuk, God sent the Chaldeans to march through the land and dispense judgment to His people. The Lord describes this enemy to the prophet by calling the Chaldeans "... that bitter and hasty nation...; ... terrible and dreadful; more fierce than evening wolves; they shall come all for violence; they shall gather the captives as the sand" (Habakkuk 1:6-11). I am sure this was one promise from God Habakkuk would have rather not heard. Yet the Lord, in His mercy, was taking Habakkuk to the place where he could no longer rest in himself!

Trouble serves this purpose. Adversity exposes the inadequacy of self-reliance, therefore, trial and distress are not far from God's rest. In our difficulty, God's objective is to demonstrate the insufficiency of a circumstance – dependent life, and the complete sufficiency of His life. In the natural, you usually relax when your circumstances are favorable. But will you rest when these circumstances become adverse? Only in Christ can you do so.

The Way and the Destination of the adverse circumstances is Jesus.

Adversity reveals the total sufficiency of His Life while at the same time exposing our heart's "rest less" condition.

Adversity reveals our heart to <u>us</u>...our misplaced trust in temporal things...the trust we place in ourselves...the uselessness of self-sufficiency.

As He exposes our heart to us He also reveals what we believe about Him... "Surely, God must be angry with me because of sin. Trouble is evidence that His hand is against me".

Blessedly, the fire of adversity burns all the dross away until He, alone, is revealed. Finally, we see who we <u>really</u> are and Who He <u>really</u> is! We are emptied of all strength and filled with His strength. We are rendered loveless, hopeless, faithless and find Him to be our Love, Hope and Faith.

As He reveals who we <u>really</u> are and Who He <u>really</u> is, we enter His rest. His Life, His Love, His Rest...is ours.

As Habakkuk heard of the adversity that was coming he said, "...my belly trembled, my lips quivered at the voice; rottenness entered into my bones, and I trembled in myself, that I might <u>rest</u> in the day of trouble..." (Habakkuk 3:16).

Habakkuk rested not because things got better. He rested because the Lord over the adversity was the Lord who loved him. Resting in the Lord does not mean that your knees aren't knocking, your legs aren't wobbling, and your heart is not trembling. The truth is, you cannot rest in God until you have wobbled and trembled in your own effort. Habakkuk says, "... I trembled in myself, that I might rest..." <u>The recognition of your own inadequacy reveals the total adequacy of Jesus in the midst of your trouble. This revelation is rest</u>.

How do you come to the place of rest? In Exodus 33:14, the Lord said, "... My presence shall go with thee, and I will give thee rest." Rest is a promise. Rest is a gift. Rest is a person. You will never rest by performing for God, but by receiving from the Lord Himself. In His presence your trouble will not trouble you, "and <u>His rest</u> shall be glorious" (Isaiah 11:10).

You stand confident in the presence of God because of one thing, the righteousness of Jesus.

THE FAITH OF JESUS

☙

"And being found in Him, not having mine own righteousness, which is of the law, but that which is through <u>the faith of Christ</u>, the righteousness which is of God by Faith" (Philippians 3:9).

By holy initative, God "...commendeth His love toward us... while we were yet sinners..." (Romans 5:8). Faith in Jesus, redemption and salvation, was a process begun in you by God. He brought you to the place of recognized need, then repentance, and introduced you to the Way, the Truth, and Life by Whom you came to the Father. By faith <u>in</u> Jesus as the only way to be saved and made righteous before God, you were not merely changed or improved. You were crucified...deceased! (Galatians 2:20).

But God did not leave you dead in Christ. Jesus was resurrected from the dead. He is alive and still walks by faith. Of you Jesus said, "...he that believeth in me, though he were dead, yet shall he live" (John 11:25). You who are saved by faith <u>in</u> Jesus are now called to live life by the faith <u>of</u> Jesus. "... I live; yet not I, but Christ liveth in me; <u>and the life which I now live in the flesh I live by the faith of the Son of God</u>..."(Galatians 2:20).

When you are storm tossed and the trials of life press down upon you, understand that as a believer you are no longer dependent upon your faith <u>in</u> Jesus for His deliverance. You now live by the faith _of_ Jesus. The storm poses no threat. He is Lord of the storms. He is Lord of trials and tribulations. He is Lord of the predicament and circumstance. Since you no longer live outside of Christ, you are no longer threatened. You are no longer in jeopardy. You are not at risk. You are more than a conqueror _through_ Him, not because of your faith _in_ Him, but because of the faith _of_ Him Who resides in you! Christ lives in you (Galatains 2:20). The mysterious riches of God's glory is "...Christ in you the hope of glory" (Colossians 1:27). His eternal, internal Presence in you enables Him to live His life in you and through you, not by faith _in_ Him, but by the faith _of_ Him, who saved you and keeps you.

It is "by the faith _of_ Christ" that we continually receive the righteousness, which is of God. "Even the righteousness of God which is by the faith _of_ Jesus Christ unto all and upon all them that believe..." (Roman 3:22). It is by _His_ faith, the faith of Christ, that we live.

IN LIKENESS OF LIZARDS

☙

Proverbs 30:28 (NIV) (Amplified) tells us that, "A lizard can be seized with the hand, yet it is found in King's palaces."

With a family history in the pest control business, I can attest to the fact that lizards are quite adept at locating in lofty places. In spite of his great wisdom, King Solomon still marveled that a lizard could establish his dwelling place in the King's palace. His dismay undoubtedly came because the lizard seemed misplaced. The palace of the King is a place for gold, silver, fashionable linen, jewels, royalty, fine food, and elegant furnishings. It is not that lizards never entered the palace, but when exposed, they were severely dealt with as trespassers.

I cannot verify that the King's administrator contracted for monthly pest control service, but I can be reasonably certain that some appointee had the responsibility of eradicating the embarrassing pest. A King's palace is no place for lizards.

Think of the royal palace of heaven. Marvel at the wondrous gathering of the despised, rejected, disgraced, obscure, indistinct, and persecuted throng of saints. Here we have those "not accepting deliverance, that they might obtain a better resurrection; "And others had trial of cruel mockings and scourgings, yea moreover, of bonds and imprisonment...stoned...sawn asunder...tested...

slain…destitute, afflicted, tormented…they wandered in deserts, and in mountains, and in dens and caves…" (Hebrews 11:35-38). Included in this vast gathering in the King's palace are, Rahab the harlot, Jacob the liar, Judah the adulterer, David the murderer, incestuous Lot, the adulterous Bathsheba, Saul (Paul) the persecutor of the church, and many, many more just like them…and you and I. All of these, in the natural, would seem out of place in the King of King's palace. "…But where sin abounded, grace did much more abound" (Romans 5:20). What a testimony to the results of grace at work. "But God,…Even when we were dead in sins, hath made us alive together with Christ (by grace ye are saved), And hath raised us up together, and made us sit together in heavenly places in Christ Jesus…" (Ephesians 2:4-6). When God's grace is your only qualification, you then qualify to be found in the King's palace. No other qualification is needed, or accepted. The Lord claims by grace those who have no claim to grace. Thus, when you consider those "sanctified lizards" who have access to the courts of the King, you will find the <u>unwanted</u>, who, like Jesus (John 1:10-11), were rejected by men; the <u>unlikely</u>, who are clothed by the compassion of the Almighty Father; the <u>unrighteous</u>, of whom God says in Hebrews 8:12, "I will be merciful to their unrighteousness, and their sins and iniquities I will remember no more."

The inhabitants of heaven will also include the <u>unlovely</u>. Those who understand that "…though the outward man perish, yet the inward man is renewed day by day" (2 Corinthians 4:16). The <u>unloved</u> will comprise a portion of heaven's populace. "Marvel not, my brethren, if the world hate you" (1 John 3:13). Another saintly lizard of heavenly residence will be the <u>unknown</u>. Lizards can live long lives undetected, obscure, and hidden. Yet they can enjoy the blessings of the palace and all its accouterments. Who can name the rope holders who saved Paul's life in Damasus (Acts 9:25)? How much is known of Shamgar, of whom it is said delivered Israel with an ox goad (Judges 3:31)? Can you name the worthless men who became mighty warriors who joined Jephthah in the land of Tob (Judges 11:3)?

Heaven is filled with the unwanted, the unlikely, the unrighteous, the unloved, the unlovely, and the unknown. May God remind you when you are tempted to criticize, despise, judge, ridicule, alienate, or reject another believer, that if you would see these saints as your Father sees them, you would surely marvel at their beauty. Besides, your sin and failures qualify you too as the "unlikely", the "unrighteous", and the "unlovely", inhabiting the courts of the King only by God's grace. It is the mystery of grace.

In the day of King Solomon, the unwanted, unloved, unlovely, lizard had to secretly sneak his way into the King's palace. He knew that being exposed would result in certain death. As a believer, you may "Enter into His gates with thanksgiving, and into His courts with praise" (Psalms 100:4). You need not fear being exposed, for you are a son of the King (1 John 3:2)! Your invitation as a son is simple. "Let us therefore, come boldly unto the throne of grace, that we may obtain mercy, and find grace to help in time of need" (Hebrews 4:16).

"It is difficult to remain devoted utterly to the person of the Lord Jesus Christ. In the midst of acclaim, in the midst of the flush of accomplishment, we are in danger of falling in love with our work more than with Him for Whom it is being done."

Paul Billheimer
"The Mystery of God's Providence"

WINNING

"...let us run with patience the race that is set before us..." (Hebrews 12:1).

As conflict rears its ugly head in many churches, sides are taken, battle lines are drawn, and relationships are severed. Strife produces bitterness instead of brokenness during these evangelical meltdowns. Likewise, in the Christian family setting, divorce rates parallel those of non-Christian families very closely. In these conflicts, we often apply an unholy criteria to answer the question, " who wins?" We are tempted to measure the concept of winning by standards that contradict the nature of God.

Do you win if the majority agrees with your view? Is winning a battle defined by who stays at a church and who leaves? Is custody of the children or financial considerations a reliable measurement of victory?

If you desire to win, you will need to redefine the term "win". You cannot win battles until you...win Christ..."(Philippians 3:8). In fact, winning Christ empowers you to win every argument. You can only "win Christ" when you suffer the loss of all other things. You must count everyone of them as refuse. Gaining the upper hand is dung. Having the last word is dung. Having a groundswell of support by the majority to affirm you is rubbish. Exalting your position or principle to the sacrificing of relationships is counted as loss. Winning Christ begins with a willingness to lose the battle. "Yea doubtless, and I count all things but loss for the excellency of the knowledge of Christ Jesus, my Lord; for whom I have suffered the loss of all things, and do count them but dung, that I may win Christ" (Philippians 3:8).

You win when you value the relationship more than your reasoning. You win when you value the person more than a principle. You win when you value the individual more than ideas that justify the certainty of your narrow convictions. To define winning any other way is to lose.

Jesus plus something equals nothing. Jesus plus nothing equals everything.

IN LIEU OF PROMINENCE

♛

"Then the disciples took him by night, and let him down by the wall in a basket" (Acts 9:25).

As an observer and participator in church life, I am reminded that the overwhelming majority of believers are of little prominence. I remain hard pressed to name the intercessors, those who fasted, the anonymous givers, the unacknowledged warriors, and the unidentified encouragers and restorers. My inability to name the nameless or even categorize their activity speaks of their obscurity.

It is not the activities and attitudes done in obscurity that determine real motive. It is the obscurity itself that discloses our heart. Will you be satisfied for Christ alone to exalt you? Will you be satisfied should he choose not to do so at all?

One of the great works of God in your life is His diminishing of you. John the Baptist testified of this reality when he said, "He (Jesus) must increase, but I must decrease" (John 3:30). Notice, John did not say that he, John, should increase. He acknowledged that he must decrease. John saw this process as necessary for his life to magnify the life of Jesus. John overcame the lie that the greater <u>his</u> visibility and activity in the Kingdom of God, the greater the Kingdom of God.

Resistance is the natural response to anyone or anything that would serve to decrease you. You will encounter a strong urge to rise up. You will be inclined to pursue your own advancement, failing to discern that to go upward in the Kingdom of God, you must go down. The modern day church has been deceived into believing that the largest, loudest, and otherwise most obvious ministry must have God's approval and anointing. But is this conclusion consistent with the life of Jesus?

The opportunities obscurity brings to you are both numerous and beneficial. Many unnoticed, unknown, unsung, remote, hidden, covered, irrelevant, and trivial have known the mighty anointing of the Lord. Within the Kingdom of God, the human instrument is never the focus. The focal point is always Jesus. This is the great opportunity of your obscurity. You become privileged to glorify Jesus in your inconspicuous condition.

Jesus enumerates other benefits in John 12:24, when He said, "...except a seed... fall into the ground and die, it abideth alone; but if it die, it bringeth forth much fruit." You, the seed, must descend, diminish, disappear, then die. This process of decrease, of obscurity, is God's method of preparing you for the spirit-filled life that ultimately "brings forth much fruit."

Your decline and ultimate fruitfulness is aided by life's fertilization process. Your disappearance is furthered along by the "dung" of life that is piled upon you within the providence of God. Although the benefit of these events is not always readily apparent, heaven will record the process as one of the opportunities for growth that obscurity brings to you.

How far must you decrease so that Christ in you might increase? How far did Christ decrease? He "...made Himself of no reputation..." And ...he humbled Himself and became obedient unto death..." (Philippians 2:7-8). The Seed of David descended, decreased, diminished, and disappeared to the extreme of dying, so that He might bring forth much fruit. You, believer, are the fruit of His demise. Your claim to membership in God's family is ongoing proof that Jesus continues to make Himself of no reputation. Paul Billheimer has often shared these words, "He laid aside His reputation, when He came and stood by me."

To you unsung mothers and fathers; to you unknown intercessors and encouragers; to you that restore the fallen with gentleness; to you remote shepherds and teachers; to you evangelists who labor in the seemingly insignificant arenas; to all of you who are the obscure, the hidden, the removed, the secluded, the concealed, and the unseen...God engineered obscurity presents you with some wonderful opportunities. Fame will often result in the praises of men. However, as the Father exalted Jesus from His death on the cross (Philippians 2:9), <u>He</u> will one day exalt you in your humility. "Humble yourselves, therefore, under the mighty hand of God, that He may exalt you in due time..." (I Peter 5:6). Jesus said, "...whosoever shall exalt himself shall be abased; and he that shall humble himself shall be exalted" (Matthew 23:12).

Believer, rest and rejoice in the fact that you are well-known by Jesus. Jesus said "I am the good shepherd, and know my sheep..." (John 10:14). To be distracted or disheartened by a lack of prominence among men is to struggle with a lesser thing.

You have no need to be right when the need to be righteous has been met.

ACCOUNTING FOR GOD'S GENEROSITY

"If he hath wronged thee, or oweth thee anything, put that on mine account" (Philemon 18).

The Lord has His own method of accounting. This method is an affront to men's thinking, and as it is applied to the situations of life, often causes resentment and anger toward God.

Matthew 20:1-16 is a story of God's accounting procedure. Workers, hired early one morning, agreed to work for a prescribed wage. After three hours, and then after six hours, the employer hired more workers. At the eleventh hour, just before the end of the day, he found more laborers whom he employed. At the end of the workday the lord of the vineyard told the supervisor to pay all the laborers. The supervisor did as directed. Each laborer was paid an equal amount. Needless to say, those who had labored all day in the heat "...murmured against the householder..." (verse 11).

In this parable Jesus says, "Is it not lawful to do what I will with mine own? Is thine eye evil, because I am good? So the last shall be first, and the first last..." (Matthew 20:15-16a).

God's grace never operates on a reward-for-work-done basis. His grace is generous beyond all measure. His grace always far exceeds our accomplishments.

In Matthew 19:27, Peter reminds Jesus that he had forsaken all to follow the Lord. He then asks Jesus "What will there be for me because of my sacrifice?" Jesus promises a hundredfold return, and promises that Peter "...shall inherit everlasting life" (Matthew 19:29). Jesus was assuring him that in the Kingdom of Heaven, God's accounting system was not based on Peter's sacrifice, but on His grace and goodness.

Have you ever jealously resented the demonstration of God's goodness and mercy generously given to an individual you determined to be undeserving? Me, too. The Law demands that people be rewarded on the basis of their performance instead of God's promises. How foolish you would be to demand that the Lord reward you based upon what you worked for or earned. The laborers in Matthew 20 who worked the longest amount of time wanted a reward system based on performance. They murmured against a God who dared not use man's method of accounting. They wanted a wage for their labor. <u>To demand to get what you deserve is to ask God for far less than He desires to give you</u>.

God delights in giving gifts not wages. Grace is a gift and is never earned by obedience. In fact, it was at the place of rebellion and disobedience that you received grace for salvation. According to the balance sheet of God's accounting system, "For what shall it profit a man if he gain the whole world and lose his own soul?" (Mark 8:36). <u>There is no profit in self-effort</u>. Man's accounting may persuasively argue that "God helps a man who helps himself; "but He does not. He has made no promise to do so. Being "... justified by grace...", and grace alone, enables you "... to maintain good works..." that "...are good and profitable unto men." (Titus 3:7-8); "not by works of righteousness which we have done, but according to His mercy..." (Titus 3:5a).

Martin Luther, in his exposition of Deuteronomy 8:17-18 said this: "... <u>blessings</u> ... at times come to us through our labors, and at times without our labors, but never <u>because</u> of our labors; for <u>God always gives them because of His undeserved mercy</u>."

Forsake the wage earner's mentality! Receive the gift of grace. Then you'll live abundantly and profitably... And that is the bottom line.

"If you hear a teaching and feel as though it were unattainable in your condition, you have only heard half the message. You missed the grace which is always resident in the heart of God's truth. Truth without grace is only half-truth. Remember this always: Grace and truth are realized in Jesus Christ (Jn 1:17). What God's truth demands, His grace will provide".

Francis Frangipane
"Holiness, Truth, and The Presence of God"

GRACE AND TRUTH

"And the Word was made flesh, and dwelt among us (and we beheld His glory, the glory as of the only begotten of the Father), full of <u>grace</u> and <u>truth</u>" (John 1:14).

Jesus is the full declaration of the Father. He is full of both <u>grace</u> and <u>truth</u>. The <u>truth</u> is that under the law God demands righteousness <u>from</u> you. By grace, He freely gives righteousness <u>to</u> you through Christ Jesus. "And of His fullness have all we received, and grace for grace" (John 1:16). Both "...grace and truth came by Jesus Christ" (John 1:17).

The way to knowing God is Jesus, Who is full of both <u>grace</u> and <u>truth</u>. The life of Christ does not consist of "a little of both", but <u>all of both</u>. Jesus "... hath declared Him (the Father)" (John 1:18). Grace and truth are inseparable in Jesus' explanation of the Father. Both are equally necessary. If you did not know the truth about the righteous demands of a Holy Father, you would have no sense of your need for grace. If you didn't know about the wonderful love and favor of your Father, Who frees you from the liability of the law through Jesus' righteousness, the hopelessness of failure would be overwhelming.

Francis Frangipane wrote, "If you hear a teaching and feel as though it were unattainable in your condition, you have only heard half the message. You missed the grace which is always resident in the heart of God's truth. Truth without grace is only half-true. Remember this always: Grace and truth are realized in Jesus Christ. <u>What God's truth demands, His grace will provide</u>."

God's truth makes His grace a necessity. His grace makes truth a delight. In Jesus, both are the ingredients for fullness of life.

AN "OUGHT TO" MENTALITY

Early in our Christian journey we are taught that we should be pleasing to God. You please God by doing good things for Him. Of course you perform diligently, faithfully, and steadfastly. The activities that please God most are praying, witnessing, giving, worshipping, interceding, and being holy. Each of us understands that our inability to perform these tasks with some degree of success grieves the Holy Spirit, causes some fellow believers to stumble, and marks us as a failure. We constantly feel the need to do better.

Great freedom will come your way as you discover that <u>you cannot live the Christian life</u>. <u>The good news is that you are not required to do so</u>. God knows this, so He freely offers you Jesus, Who does <u>in</u> you and <u>through</u> you what He desires. Galatians 2:20 reminds us, "I am crucified with Christ; nevertheless I live; yet not I, but Christ liveth in me; and the life which I <u>now</u> live in the flesh I live by the faith of the Son of God, who loved me and gave Himself for me." Notice, I do not live by faith <u>in</u> Jesus. I am now living literally by the faith <u>of</u> Jesus.

<u>The Christian life is the life of Jesus</u>. Who is more qualified to live the Christian life than Jesus? He is Life. "I am...the life"... John 14:6. He is grace defined. He is our ability to know and do the will of the Father. Jesus doesn't merely help us in our quest to know God. Jesus enables us to both know, and please, the Father, "And of His fullness have all we received, and grace for grace" (John 1:16).

External regulation will never produce internal righteousness. Only the presence of Jesus can do this work. Thus, Jesus saves us from ourselves.

The presence of any diligence, faithfulness, holiness, righteousness, steadfastness or Godliness in our lives is testimony of the ability of <u>Jesus</u> to live the Christian life, not us. To <u>Him</u> be all honor and glory.

YOUR DOING VERSUS YOUR BEING

♛

Does God require you to be faithful to His calling upon your life for you to know success in the Kingdom of God? To answer this question correctly, you first must understand that to which God calls you.

The Lord never gives you an assignment in His kingdom that can be accomplished in your own strength. Likewise, He will not choose any task that requires you to "give it all you've got", plus God. Whatever His desire is, be assured that "...<u>it is God who worketh</u> in you both to will and to do of His pleasure" (Philippians 2:13). Your performance, good or bad, in response to His call, brings Him no good pleasure. It is <u>His</u> pleasure and delight to do <u>His</u> work both in you, then through you. <u>The legitimacy of your calling is</u> <u>based upon the fact that the Lord is faithful to your calling...not you</u>. Success, apart from His working, does not legitimize it. Failure does not make it illegitimate. Illegitimacy is your attempting to do that which only God can do. This is pride, which God resists. "Faithful is He that calleth you, who also will do it" (I Thessalonians 5:24). "I will cry unto God most high; unto God who performeth all things for me" (Psalms 57:2).

To view your calling by God as an assignment that requires activity on your part, is to miss God. God's calling upon your life involves your <u>being</u> rather than your doing. Your "high calling" (Philippians 3:14), your "holy calling" (2 Timothy 1:9), and your "heavenly calling" (Hebrews 3:1), is one of being, not doing. You can never do enough to accomplish what God the Father has chosen you to be.

Your doing cannot result in you becoming a child of God, because salvation is "not of works, lest any man should boast" (Ephesians 2:9). Your doing cannot make you a son of God (I John 3:2); your doing cannot make you righteous (2 Corinthians 5:21); your doing cannot reconcile you to God (2 Corinthians 5:18); your doing cannot justify you (Romans 3:24). What you do may often be of your own choosing and at you own initiation. But what you are in Christ, is a work only the Lord Himself can do. He defines your being. His work at work in you is your calling. God's calling upon you is not a calling to do; it is rather, a calling to be.

Sin is similar. Sin is not just wrong doing. Sin is wrong being. As a sinner, your being needs changing, not merely your doing. When your being is changed, your activities change. The high calling is not to do better; it is to be made a new creature.

Your success in the kingdom of God will never be measured by your faithfulness to His Calling. You cannot be faithful. Your efforts are futile. God's calling upon you is so high, so holy, so enormous, that it is a call that He and He alone can faithfully accomplish. To Him be all glory.

BUT WHAT ABOUT OBEDIENCE?

What is the essence of obeying God, and where does the desire to do so come from? The answer to both questions is expressed in one word…Jesus.

Obedience is not a work you do. Obedience is a work that Jesus does in us and ultimately through us by the Holy Spirit. Obedience is not accomplished when we have achieved something for God, but when we have <u>received</u> from God. <u>You never achieve anything for God beyond what you have received from God</u>. The true measure of anything accomplished in the kingdom of God is the faithfulness of "He that calleth you, <u>who also will do it</u>" (I Thessalonians 5:24).

<u>Faith then, and ultimately obedience, is simply Christ in you responding to, and relating to the Father.</u>

Obedience then becomes a testimony to <u>His</u> mightiness, not yours. The focus of our obedience is <u>always Him</u>, not us. It is not "how we are doing." Rather, it is, "what is God doing." After all, "For it is God who worketh <u>both</u> to <u>will</u> and to <u>do</u> of His good pleasure" (Philippians 2:13).

Obedience should never be defined by volume of activity in our lives. It is better defined or measured by the <u>life of Jesus</u> resident in our lives. You may be generating a great deal of activity for God, and in all likelihood, have not obeyed.

You are constantly receiving something in your life. Obedience will be defined by how much of what you receive looks and acts like Jesus.

A.B. Simpson once said, "God is not seeking so much to have us do more for Him, as to take more from Him, and thus of His Own shall we give back to Him again."

<u>Obedience is not the way to Jesus. Jesus is the way to obedience.</u>

A BELIEVER'S OBEDIENCE AND DISOBEDIENCE

"I will cry unto God most high; unto God that performeth all things for me" (Psalms 57:2).

To obey the commands of Holy God is a noble thing. Our effort to obey does not make this venture noble. Our attempt makes it futile. Only Jesus makes obedience a noble activity, because only Jesus can succeed at it. With this revelation, the eternal becomes internal. The pressure of having to perform is lifted, and you rest in the obedience of Jesus as the sole basis of your good standing with the Father.

<u>The believer's obedience is Jesus</u>. Everything Jesus accomplishes is eternal. Everything is done in response only to the Father ...nothing more, nothing less, and nothing else.

Philippians 2:7-8, when referring to Jesus, Paul said "But made Himself of no reputation, and took upon Him the form of a servant, and was made in the likeness of men: And being found in fashion as a man, He humbled Himself, and became <u>obedient unto death</u>, even the death of the cross".

"Obedience unto death" is the only act of total obedience...that level of obedience that completely satisfies God. Nothing less will do. Only Jesus is capable of "obedience unto death, even the death of the cross."

For the children of God, <u>self-reliance is disobedience</u>. To believe that Father God loves you, approves of you, and accepts you for any other reason than Jesus, is to be deceived.

God often permits His children to live in self-effort and self-reliance. He does so that He might lead you to Himself. Self-reliance is so contrary to being "...a new creature in Christ..." (II Cor. 5:17), that it cannot co-exist with joy, peace, and rest. The self-reliant state of disobedience will run its weary and frustrating course. The beleaguered, burnt out believer will cry out, "I can't live the Christian life!" Soon the revelation of the Life of Christ, willing, doing, and pleasing the Father, brings peace, joy, rest, and restoration. Father God has reserved these works of righteousness for Jesus alone. The good news is, Jesus performs <u>all</u> things for you!

THE WRONG TIME FOR GRACE

"And he said, Tomorrow…" (Exodus 8:10).

It has often been said that there is a right time and a wrong time for everything. I am not convinced that this statement is true, only that it is commonly proclaimed.

Yet there is most assuredly a right time and a wrong time to walk in the liberty freely offered to us by God's grace through His Son Jesus. The right time is now. The wrong time is tomorrow. "Now we, brethren,…are the children of promise" (Galatians 4:28). Not tomorrow, but now. "Beloved, now are we the sons of God…" (I John 3:2).

Instead of attempting to live under the oppressive bondage of men's rules, regulations, and expectations, you would think that believers would rush into the life of liberty, and stand fast, daring anyone to preach or teach "…another gospel…" (Galatians 1:6). "Stand fast, therefore, in the liberty with which Christ hath made us free, and be not entangled again with the yoke of bondage" (Galatians 5:1). Yet, confusion, doubt, fear, depression, and many other struggles plague God's people because we regularly choose to have our lives manipulated and influenced by the doctrines of men, the customs of a religious society, and the convictions of brethren who establish rules and regulations that falsely judge true spirituality.

In Exodus 8 we are told that Pharaoh was plagued by an

abundance of frogs (Exodus 8:3). There was no place free from frogs. Frogs were in the beds, the ovens, the food, and on the people. Everything and everyone was covered with frogs. In his misery Pharaoh told Moses to "...Entreat the Lord, that He may take away the frogs from me..." (Exodus 8:8). He wanted relief. He was miserable the way he was living. Yet when Moses asked Pharaoh how quickly he wanted his freedom from what plagued him, Pharaoh gave an astonishing response. "And he said, Tomorrow..." (Exodus 8:10).

Tomorrow! Not today! Not right now! Not as soon as possible? Tomorrow? If a slimy frog took residence in your bed or oven, you would react quickly, and act decisively. Should you guard your heart less zealously? Should you discern what you hear and believe less diligently? Should you stand less vigorously against any word from men that brings you bondage and condemnation?

As Paul writes to the believers in Galatia, he is more than merely concerned. He is righteously angry regarding those who preach "...another gospel..." (Galatians 1:6), and who "...trouble believers (by) ...perverting the gospel of Christ" (1:7). Paul says let him who preaches anything but God's grace "...be accursed" (1:8). So emphatic was he, that Paul restates his position in verse 9 by saying, "...If any man preach any other gospel unto you than that ye have received, let him be accursed." Later, in Galatians 5:12 Paul says, "I would they were ever cut off who trouble you."

Guard your heart. Is what you believe the Gospel? If what you hear, read, and receive produces guilt or condemnation, it is not the Gospel of Jesus. If you are challenged to better live the Christian life so as to gain God's love and acceptance, it is not the Gospel of Jesus. Just as your justification and sanctification are never jeopardized by your performance, grace is never imperiled by your lack of trust. <u>The only thing that frustrates grace is your delay in receiving it.</u>

THE PROBLEM OF PROMISES PERFORMED

"The Lord is not slack concerning His promise…"
(2 Peter 3:9a)

It is my understanding that there are more than 7,000 promises recorded in Scripture given by God to His people. In a life span of 70 years that would calculate to more than 100 promises annually. This means there are two brand new promises per week for every week of your life. Are you receiving two promises weekly, or have you missed a few?

A promise is an agreement, a commitment, or a pledge to do something. We might call it a vow. When God makes a promise, He alone keeps His promise. We have His word on it. His word is Jesus. In fact, Jesus is a promise from God, "But the Scripture hath concluded all under sin, that the promise by faith of Jesus Christ might be given to them that believe" (Galatians 3:22). The Holy Spirit is a promise from the Father. "…that we might receive the promise of the Spirit through faith" (Galations 3:14). God's forgiveness of our sins is a promise.

Promises are given. In essence, God's promises are gifts. They are appropriated only by receiving them. There are no exceptions. What the Father decides to give you is far better than what you could ever produce for Him. Thus, you receive forgiveness. You

<u>receive</u> eternal life. You <u>receive</u> His presence. You <u>receive</u> His love, His mercy, and His grace. You do not ever obtain a promise by earning it. That is a wage. God's promises are never given to us because we have earned them or deserve them.

The value of a promise is never measured by the promise. It is measured by the reliability of the Promisor. The worth of a promise will never exceed the capability of the Promisor to perform. "The Lord is not slack concerning His promises..." (Peter 2:9).

Abraham and Sarah heard God's promise to them of a son (Genesis 15:1-6). After many years of waiting for God to perform His promise, Abraham and Sarah decided that God needed assistance...their assistance. So they embarked on a well "conceived" plan to perform the promise of God.

Let their error be a lesson for us all. <u>God's promises can only be received, not performed</u>. If you succumb to the urge to produce one of God's promises, you most certainly will produce...an Ishmael. And once Ishmael is birthed, he will demand to be fed, watered, pampered, and nurtured. How many times have we birthed these Ishmael programs and structures and activities, only to find that the demands are burdensome, and the yoke upon us is heavy?

There is one final caution regarding our relationship to the promises of God. A legalistic mentality will always take a promise of God and turn it into a requirement. Most of the time, what men require you to do for God is the very thing that God Himself has promised to do on your behalf. Acts 1:8 says, "... and ye shall be witnesses unto Me...". That's a promise, not a requirement. As we learn to <u>receive</u> the promises of God, the effect will be a witness far better and far beyond what man could ever require of you.

The Lord God is not only a promise making and promise keeping God, but He is also a covenant (promise) remembering Father. "Nevertheless, He regarded their affliction, when He heard their cry; and <u>He remembered for them</u> His covenant..." (Psalms 106:44-45a). We can neither make covenant (promises) nor keep covenant (promises) with God. Moreover, we can not even remember His covenant (promise) for ourselves. The Promisor does ALL!

ON BEING A WITNESS

"…And ye shall be witnesses unto Me…" Acts 1:8

Mention the phrase "you ought to be a witness for Christ" to many believers, and the reaction to the suggestion is most often fear and anxiety. Visions of angry people rejecting both you and your God seem more real than life itself. And yet to not witness is to ignore one of the cornerstone commands of God. Really? Were you to consider witnessing for Jesus, as a command, you would calculate and contemplate the effort needed to achieve obedience.

Were you to consider witnessing for Jesus as <u>His</u> promise, You will find that His "…yoke is easy, and (His) burden is light" (Matthew 11:30). His enabling presence makes it so. You will have no need to <u>make</u> it happen. Your witness will be a work <u>He</u> does. The fact of the matter is that as a believer, you <u>are</u> a witness. When Jesus stated in Acts 1:8 that "…ye shall be witnesses unto Me…" He was not issuing a command. He was proclaiming a promise! You are not under a mandatory injunction from Jesus to witness, or else. You are the recipient of a wonderful promise that as you know Jesus, He, frees you to be all that He has designed and designated you to be. You <u>are</u> a witness…and that is a promise.

This in no way sets aside the importance of a believer's divine intensity, or holy zeal. "And whatsoever ye do, do it heartily, as to the Lord…" (Colossians 3:23). But you must ask, of what thing am

I zealous? For whom is my intensity spent? Your attempt to perform a promise of God that only He can perform through you is misspent zeal.

The Holy Spirit of God, Who bears witness <u>to</u> you of Jesus, will likewise bear witness <u>in</u> you of Jesus. He then bears witness <u>through</u> you to others. "But ye shall <u>receive</u> power, after that the Holy Ghost is come upon you: and <u>ye shall be witnesses unto me</u>..." (Acts 1:8). Jesus recognized that an effective witness through you is not possible until He reveals the witness of the Holy Spirit to you.

"Who is he that overcometh the world, but he that believeth that Jesus is the Son of God? This is He that came by water and blood, even Jesus Christ; not by water only, but by water and blood. <u>And it is the Spirit that beareth witness, because the Spirit is truth</u>. For there are three that bear record in heaven, the Father, the Word, and the Holy Spirit; and these three are One.

And there are three that bear witness in earth, the Spirit, and the water, and the blood; and these three agree in One. If we receive the witness of men, the witness of God is greater; for this is the witness of God, which He hath testified of His Son. He that believeth on the Son of God <u>hath the witness in himself</u>..." (I John 5:5-10A).

As you journey day by day, opportunity will abound for you to observe the workings of God in and through your life. As you receive the fullness of joy that Jesus promises, it will shine forth in a sad and lonely world. In essence, your cup will overflow. Your peace that passes all understanding will bring His peace to troubled souls. Jesus will flow through you to be light in dark places. Your place of rest will not go unnoticed in a restless world. As he equips you with Himself to live without fear, the inhabitants of a fearful world will be watching.

Do not fall into the trap of trying to become what you already are. <u>You are a witness.</u> <u>That's His promise.</u>

HOW TO ACCESS GRACE

꿏

"By whom also we have access by faith into this grace..." Romans 5:2

Grace is obtained only by faith. You simply believe the favor of God is readily available through Jesus alone, then receive it. Conversely, unbelief denies you access to grace. For unbelief will cause either one of two things to happen in your life. You will become convinced that you must perform in order to earn God's favor and approval, or you will allow yourself to be convinced that your sin always obstructs God's flow of grace. Neither is true.

God's promises do not come through keeping the law. They flow by and through Jesus. Roman 5:1-2 says, "Therefore, being justified by faith, we have peace with God, through our Lord Jesus Christ, by whom also we have access by faith into this grace in which we stand..." Your sacrificial service to God does not motivate Him to give you grace. Performing for God to obtain His approval, love, or favor is itself unbelief! You are attempting to define the terms that give you access to God's grace. He has already defined access to all His benefits when He freely gave us His Son, Christ Jesus.

Likewise, your sin never obstructs the flow of God's grace to you.

Just as your performance cannot earn grace, your sin cannot keep you from grace. In fact <u>your sin spotlights your need for grace</u>! (Ephesians 2:8 "For by grace are ye saved..."). Only unbelief keeps you from experiencing God's grace.

Access to grace is by the faith of the Lord Jesus Christ. Jesus alone is God's remedy for unbelief. The Father knew from the beginning that you would fail, and that only Jesus would be steadfast, faithful, and true. Jesus not only <u>kept</u> His Father's word, He <u>is</u> His Father's word. <u>Only He can save you from the futility of either self-effort, or self-condemnation.</u> Only <u>in Him</u> do you have access to grace.

YOU CAN'T DRIVE YOUR CAR TO NASSAU

♛

"And if by grace, then is it no more of works; otherwise grace is no more grace. But if it be of works, then is it no more grace..." (Romans 11:6).

You cannot drive your car to Nassau because the way a vehicle is designed will not permit it. It is designed to run on solid ground.

You are designed to "run" on grace. Every believer acknowledges that their salvation was by grace (Ephesians 2:8-10). But soon after conversion, most Christians become absolutely convinced that successful Christian living comes only by hard work and through much effort.

God's mind about grace is made up. It is His plan and design for us to <u>live</u> by grace, instead of limiting the work of grace in us for salvation only.

Grace in us is the tool the Father uses to define life. Instead of our <u>being</u> coming out of our <u>doing</u>, our <u>doing</u> comes forth out of our <u>being</u>. Our identity doesn't come out of what we do for God. Our identity comes out of who Christ is in us.

The scripture tells us that we are a new species, a new creation. We haven't been re-designed, or had the "once-over." We have been re-born.

Duty no longer motivates the new creation. Grace (the presence of Jesus in us that enables us to know and do the will of God) does. When obligation to duty takes the place of receiving grace, our joy is quenched.

Grace provokes you to no longer seek to receive what you have earned. Instead, we receive Him and all He is. Grace ushers you beyond desiring what you deserve, to desiring Him, and Him alone. There is no longer a need to be recognized, rewarded, or honored for what we have done for God. You see what He has done for you. You are free to enjoy life's journey. Soon your passion will be to know more than His hand. You will desire to know His heart.

Believers have been born again to "run" on grace. God's mind is made up. He likes it His way.

"God is much more interested in what we are than in what we do, in what we become than in what we achieve. If failure works better than success to make us unselfish, considerate, sympathetic, and helpful to others, if it matures us in agape love, then God may permit failure because our eternal promotion is involved."

Paul Billheimer
"The Mystery of God's Providence"

HANDLING DISGRACE WITH GRACE

۝

"Wash me thoroughly from mine iniquity, and cleanse me from my sin" (Psalms 51:2).

Failure is the prerequisite to receiving God's grace. You cannot receive any measurable quantity of grace without the sense of your own need.

What two things do David, Samson, Jacob, Lot, Judah, Moses, Rahab, Bathsheba, and you and I have in common? Each one of the Biblical characters had a life marred with some significant disgrace, and each individual had an encounter with the redeeming and restoring grace of God.

A glance at Matthew 1 reveals the genealogy of Jesus. Within that lineage we find the original scoundrel, Jacob. Judah, who had an adulterous encounter with his daughter-in-law, is next in line…His daughter-in-law, Tamar, and one of the sons born of her relationship with Judah, Perez, are also there.

A closer look at Matthew 1 reveals the names of Rahab, the Jericho harlot, David the murderer, and Bathsheba, the woman with whom David had his well-publicized affair. Each one of these disgraced failures were purposefully selected by Omniscient God to be the forebearers of His Son!

Is God condoning sin? Has license taken the place of liberty? Is there no better evidence that rules and strictly enforced regulations for believers are the better way?

Romans 5:20-21 resoundingly responds, "Moreover, the law entered, that the offense might abound. But where sin abounded, grace did much more abound; That as sin hath reigned unto death, even so might grace reign through righteousness unto eternal life by Jesus Christ, our Lord."

Man handles your failure and disgrace with criticism, alienation, and condemnation. God's response to that same disgrace is to freely offer you Himself, by and through Jesus.

"Therefore, as by the offense of one judgment came upon <u>all</u> men to condemnation, even so by the righteousness of one the free gift came upon all men unto justification of life. For as by one man's disobedience many were made sinners, so by the obedience of one shall many be made righteous" (Romans 5:18,19).

For believers, failure is neither fatal or final. The issue never has been "have you failed." The answer to that is settled. The issue is have you received what God freely offers in response to your failure. When you understand that your failure is the pre-requisite to receiving grace, a time will come when you will be able to rejoice in your failure. After all, God's grace abounds much more than any disgrace we will ever know. Grace assuredly abounds instead of your failure, but also, and always, at the point of your failure.

Fear will hide the true purpose of failure… to be the opportunity for your loving Father to flood your soul with an outpouring of Himself!

WOUNDED OYSTERS AND DIVINE DELIVERANCE

"He healeth the broken in heart, and bindeth up their wounds" (Psalms 147:3).

Does God sometimes allow His children to be wounded because of their sins? No. Never. God chose Jesus to be wounded for your sin. Jesus "...was wounded for our transgressions..." (Isaiah 53:5); and "...it pleased the Lord to bruise Him..."(Isaiah 5:10). You will be wounded for sure, but your wounding will never be because of your sin. Wounding serves a higher purpose. You will be graced with the privilege of knowing Christ in "...the fellowship of His sufferings..." (Philippians 3:10) as the Lord fashions and conforms you to the image of His Son (Romans 8:20). As "...His workmanship..." (Ephesians 2:10), your wounding is the Lord's assurance that the life of Christ goes forth in you. You will never be wounded for your sin. You will be wounded only for Christ's sake.

A pearl of great value and desirability is formed by an oyster's internal response to a wound by an irritant. Because of this provocation and injury, something very beautiful, valuable, and desirable is created that would have been impossible to have without the wound.

The Biblical account of Joseph illustrated this...Joseph's life had many occasions for woundings. His brothers sold him into slavery.

Falsely accused as he diligently served in Potipher's house, Joseph was imprisoned and forgotten for many years. Without any recorded complaining, murmuring, or accusation toward God, Joseph said in Genesis 41:52, "God has caused me to be fruitful in the land of my affliction." Having gotten better, not bitter, and fruitful, not fallen, Joseph yields quietly and confidently to the conforming work of his Lord and the "pearls" of mercy, forgiveness and love are formed.

Paul Billheimer once wrote of Joseph, "If human pity could have rescued him from the sad part of his life, the glorious part that followed would have been lost."

Your response to the perplexities of life will determine if you will pout with God, or praise Him. How you <u>behave</u> in response to your wounding is not nearly as important as what you <u>believe</u> about your affliction. Right behavior will not make you fruitful in your affliction. Believing the Lord is trustworthy takes your perplexities and makes them pearls. For some, despair and depression is the outcome of difficulty. Your Father never intended anything less than pearls as the fruit of your perplexities.

FALLEN FROM GRACE

༺༻

"Christ has become of no effect unto you, whosoever of you are justified by the law; ye are fallen from grace" (Galatians 5:4).

The phrase fallen from grace has often been linked with improper conduct...or behavior that evokes God's disfavor. It implies, in the minds of many, that one in such a state has failed to keep the commands of God, and thus has fallen from favor with God.

In Galatians 5:1, Paul encourages believers to "stand fast...in the liberty with which Christ has made us free, And be not entangled again with the yoke of bondage". What is the yoke of bondage to which Paul is referring? The yoke of bondage is a "works for approval" mentality that embraces any activity that we perform, plus Jesus, to gain God's favor. In Galatians, circumcision was the activity of choice, believing, that it, plus the work of the cross, would produce righteousness.

"Fallen from grace" describes the believer who is doing his best to keep God's laws, convinced that to the degree he succeeds, he is loved, approved, and favored by God. It is retreating from receiving His undeserved and unmerited favor into working for it.

"Fallen from grace" is not failing to keep God's laws. It is trying to keep God's laws, and believing that your work, plus Jesus' work on the cross, produces righteousness. It is not losing your salvation. It is losing your rest. It is losing confidence in the finished work of Christ on your behalf. It is struggling to <u>be</u> who you already <u>are</u>. "And you, being dead in your sins and the uncircumcision of your flesh, hath he made alive, together with him, having forgiven you all trespasses, Blotting out the handwriting of ordinances that was against us, which was contrary to us, and took it out of the way, nailing it to His cross" (Colossians 2:13-14).

There is <u>nothing</u> that you can add to your redemption. It is settled in Heaven. <u>It is finished!</u>

BONFIRES AND BURNED OUT BELIEVERS

"Behold, all ye that kindle a fire, that compass yourselves about with sparks: walk in the light of your fire, and in the sparks that ye have kindled. This shall ye have of mine hand; ye shall lie down in sorrow" (Isaiah 50:11).

"Now to him that worketh is the reward not reckoned of grace, but of debt" (Romans 4:4).

Within most churches and Christian organizations, there seems to be a constant need for workers. Rarely is the question asked, "Should I serve?" Of course you should. Don't you want to please God? Is not Christian service the best way to demonstrate your gratitude to God for your salvation? Instead, it seems that the only question is "Where should I serve?" Should I teach a class? Should I sing in the choir? Maybe the pastor is right. I should help in the nursery, then sing in the choir. Your lack of peace will soon disappear into weariness, but lack of rest sure beats feeling guilty.

The fruit of God at work in you is good works. He initiates good works. His power and presence sustains good works. Good works are His idea. You cannot accomplish good works independent from God.

If you are on a journey that requires you to initiate motion and activity for the purpose of pleasing God, you are not on the journey of His choosing. You will produce works, but they will be dead.

Dead works is the activity you're doing, or the effort you're making, in the belief that it will make you more accepted or more loved by God. Wholehearted endeavor never obligates the Lord to respond with His blessings or favor. His blessings, favor, and anointing are upon you solely because of His Son Christ Jesus. "How much more shall the blood of Christ, who through the eternal Spirit offered Himself without spot to God, purge you conscience from <u>dead works</u> to serve the living God?" (Hebrews 9:14)

According to Isaiah 50:11, sorrow is the reward of those who walk in the "light of fire" of their own creation and effort.

Good works always, without exception, begin and end with grace. They are the product of <u>His</u> effort, not yours. <u>He</u> is able to make all grace abound toward you (Roman 5:20). The good works that abound <u>from</u> you are proportionate to the measure of grace that you have <u>received</u> from Him. "<u>And God is able to make all grace abound toward you; that ye</u>, always having all sufficiency in all things, <u>may abound to every good work</u>" (2 Corinthians 9:8). The resource you need to accomplish the good work that God has designed and created for you is Jesus, who came in grace and truth (John 1:14,17). He then is your light. The life of Christ is light in abundance. He is your sufficient resource.

You may have become weary in the well intended activity of the fire building. You may have rationalized that if you are going to be light in a darkened and cold world, that you need to build a fire. To build a fire is to commit to keep it going. <u>Burnout is a sure sign that you are drawing from</u> <u>the bonfire of self-sufficiency</u>.

In your darkest hour the Lord sets before you Himself, "…a fire to give light in the night…" (Psalms 105:30) As He did for the children of Israel, He will do so for you. <u>The Lord</u> is my <u>Light</u> and my salvation…" (Psalms 27:1).

LORD, YOU ARE RIGHT

I had a change of dream
For about the nineteenth time
And the plans I've made
I've just about forgot.

I've realigned my thinking
Remembering that you're Lord
And everything that you provide
is all I've got

Chorus: You are right... strong,
            never ever wrong...
            Absolute, magnificent, and true.
            The hope of life that never fails.
            in all things... prevails;
            for those who trust in You!

The timing of your Lordship
Rarely coincides with mine,
But the peace, it always comes
when I yield.

Overcoming my ambitions,
You are right everytime;
And with Your life in mine
my emptiness is filled!

LEARNING TO LEAN

☬

Hebrews 11:21 "By Faith Jacob, when he was dying, blessed both the sons of Joseph, and worshipped, leaning upon the top of his staff".

Leaning on your own understanding (Proverbs 3:5) is the <u>natural</u> response to a circumstance or individual that requires your attention. Leaning on Jesus is the <u>supernatural</u> response to the same circumstance or person.

Jacob's name means "supplanter". Using words like liar, deceiver, and double-dealer would also be an appropriate description of him. Rarely did he come forth with a straight answer. Only occasionally was he "above board." He seemed to always leave a few details unexplained. The response of others to his wheeling and dealing was what you might expect. His <u>naturally</u> lived life evoked a <u>natural</u> response from others.

Jacob manipulated the birthright from his brother, Esau, then spent the next few years running for his life. Obtaining the birthright could not have occurred without Jacob also deceiving his father, Isaac. As Jacob lived leaning on his own understanding, the <u>natural</u> response to his predicaments was to run. He became a good runner…a long distance runner…a marathon man (Genesis 31:21).

Plenty of people hated Jacob. Jacob hated Jacob. At night he cried out to God for help, then at daybreak, he would try every possible means to solve his problems his own way. Civil war raged inside him. It is not surprising that Isaiah 41:14 says "...thou worm, Jacob..."

If you are leaning on your own understanding, and reaping a natural response from others, there is an even greater, overcoming truth. Even if you live life in the natural, your life will always evoke a <u>supernatural</u> response from God. <u>He will offer you nothing less</u>.

Jacob became Israel. The worm became a "prince with God". If you were creating a prince, you would not begin with a worm. God did. God did not love Jacob for who he was or what he was, He loved Jacob where he was...leaning on his own understanding.

As Jacob encountered God, the Lord touched Jacob's thigh and crippled him (Genesis 32:25,31). From that day forward Jacob limped noticeably. He would now be required to lean on someone else. He would never run again. He didn't have a leg to stand on. God touched Jacob at the place of his greatest strengh...where he leaned most heavily, and Jacob would never be Jacob again!

Hebrews 11:21 tells us that Jacob <u>worshipped while leaning</u>. Worship can occur at no other juncture. Worship is your response to an awesome God. Worship is the evidence that you are not leaning upon anything or anyone but Jesus.

Are you weary of leaning upon your own understanding? If so, that is a good thing. For the believer, frustration and lack of rest is the prelude to the <u>supernatural</u> response that you've longed for. Your Father will <u>not</u> leave you in the captivity of living naturally. He liberates us into supernatural living...giving us His mind...Giving us His vision...Giving us HIMSELF!

A PLEASING WALK

❧

"...And Enoch walked with God..." Genesis 5:24.

Walking is a simple, physical activity, for most. It is so easy to learn that most children walk before their first birthday. Loving parents watch their little one as wobbly first steps are taken. The inevitable falls, bumps, and cries are never viewed as failures, but necessary to the transformation of toddler to child. Daddy's strong arms pick up, comfort, and reassure the wounded one. The process is replayed over and over until walking becomes second nature.

Scripture generously details how you as a believer should walk. "Walk by faith" says 2 Corinthians 5:7. Ephesians says "walk worthy" (Ephesians 4:1), "...and walk circumspectly; upright, beyond reproach..." (Ephesians 5:15). You are directed in I Thessalonians 4:12 to "walk honestly", and in Romans 6:4 to "walk in newness of life." "Walk in the light," says I John 1:17; and in Psalms 84:11-12 you are reminded that "God rewards them that walk uprightly."

What elements must define your journey through life so that your walk pleases God? You may be tempted to conclude that the less you fall and fail, the more pleased the Lord will be with you. Scripture indicates the contrary. In fact, a walk characterized by falling seems to be necessary to a God pleasing walk. Psalms

37:23-24 tells us that, "The steps of a good man are ordered by the Lord, and he delighteth in His way. Though he fall, he shall not be utterly cast down; for the Lord upholdeth him with His hand." Your falling and failure on the journey is not only a pre-requisite to receiving mercy and grace, it likewise is necessary to pleasing God. In fact, your falling is ordered by God. God is never displeased when you fall, or fail, on your journey. He is only displeased when you fail to walk with Him.

What is the walk that pleases Him? How do you walk the walk that is pleasing to the Lord God? The answer to these questions may reside within the context of another question. The prophet Amos asks, "<u>Can two walk together, except they be agreed?</u>" (Amos 3:3).

Scripture speaks of Enoch, and of him Genesis 5:24 says, "And Enoch walked with God..." The verse goes on to say that Enoch did not die, but that "...God took him." Enoch walked with God in such a manner that death had no authority over him. What characterized Enoch's walk with God that kept death from overcoming him?

Hebrews 11:5-6 tells us that "By faith Enoch was translated that he should not see death... for before his translation he had this testimony, that he pleased God".

Enoch walked with God in a manner that pleased God. How can you have this kind of walk? Many in the Scripture are said to have <u>talked</u> with God, but only two, Enoch and Noah, are described as having <u>walked</u> with God. The secret? Enoch <u>agreed</u> with God, and in doing so, both walked with God and pleased God. For Enoch, agreeing with the Lord was not an incidental or casual event. Enoch lived three hundred years, or 109,500 days.

How often do you agree with God? Has agreeing with God become your lifestyle? (Please be minded that God's word is absolutely, unequivocally true, whether you agree with Him or not.) God is right. He is completely reliable and unmistaken in His evaluation of you. As a believer you are His son (John 1:12); He has made you accepted in the beloved (Ephesians 1:6); you are justified (just as if you had never sinned) by grace (Romans 3:24); forgiven (Colossians 1:14); blessed with all spiritual blessings in heavenly places in Christ (Ephesians 1:3); made righteous and acceptable to the Father (2 Corinthians 5:21); perfected forever and sanctified (Hebrews 10:14); without guilt or condemnation (Romans 8:1); saved from wrath through Christ (Romans 5:9); and reconciled to God by Christ Jesus (Romans 5:10-11). Do you agree with God's opinion of you? <u>Enoch pleased God because he agreed with God</u>.

Be content to agree with God in every matter, because He is right in every matter. When you agree with God you will delight in His ways (Psalms 37:23-24), regardless of where the walk takes you. Your reward is the Lord Himself. "No good thing will He withhold from them that walk uprightly" (Psalms 84:11).

FROM HIS LIPS TO YOURS

☘

"...grace is poured into thy lips; therefore God hath blessed thee forever." Psalm 45:2

As a child of the King, your name is constantly on the lips of Jesus. Jesus "...ever liveth to make intercession for them"(all believers) (Hebrews 7:25). Christ continually appears "...in the presence of God for us" (Hebrews 9:24). For centuries all have "...wondered at the gracious words which proceeded out of His mouth..."(Luke 4:22). He speaks well of you. Because of what Jesus says of you, you are accepted in the beloved (Ephesians 1:6); you are redeemed; you are made righteous and holy. Grace pours from His lips on your behalf.

From His lips unto your lips grace is poured. You are now blessed forever. As grace is poured into your lips, now let the grace of Christ come forth from your lips.

Speak only the truth to others. Speak to them and of them only what Christ would say. Let judgmentalism, strife, all curses, criticism, gossip, vain talk and repetitions be far removed from you. May you who have been blessed, bless others. May the grace that pours from the lips of Jesus into your lips find a holy channel through you until it freely flows from your lips unto others. If Jesus speaks well of a brother, should you do differently?

God hath surely blessed you forever with His favor. Can you do less to those whom He likewise cherishes? "The words of a wise man's mouth are gracious, but the lips of a fool will swallow up himself" (Ecclesiates 10:12).

Grace doesn't overlook sin, it overpowers sin.

GREAT GRACE

֎

"And with great power gave the apostles witness of the resurrection of the Lord Jesus; and great grace was upon them all" (Acts 4:33).

There are two measurements of great grace: the height of its source, and the depth of its flow. Great grace can only come from a great God. "His glory is great..." (Psalms 2:5). "...He is a great King over all the earth" (Psalms 47:2). "Great is the Lord, and greatly to be praised..." (Psalms 48:1). "...who is as great a God as our God?" (Psalms 77:13). "For the Lord is a great God, and a great King above all Gods" (Psalms 95:3). It is certain that only a great God could be the source of great grace. As the great grace of God seeks the depths of wickedness to which it is destined to flow, it becomes conspicuous by its targets. Grace becomes conspicuous because its object is so reprehensible. This was spoken of by James Hervey, (1751):

> "Where sin has abounded, says the proclamation from the court of heaven, grace doth much more abound. Manassah was a monster of barbarity, for he caused his own children to pass through the fire, and filled Jerusalem with innocent blood. Manasseh was so adept in iniquity, for he not only multiplied, and

to extravagant degree, his own sacrilegious impieties, but he poisoned the principles and perverted the manners of his subjects, making them do worse than the most detestable of the heathen idolators (see II Chron. 33). Yet, through this superabundant grace he is reformed, and becomes a child of forgiving love, an heir of immortal glory.

Behold that bitter and bloody persecutor, Saul; when, breathing out threatenings and bent upon slaughter, he worried the lambs and put to death the disciples of Jesus. The havoc he had committed, the inoffensive families he had already ruined, were not sufficient to assuage his vengeful spirit. They were only a taste, which, instead of glutting the bloodhound, made him more closely pursue the track, and more eagerly pant for destruction. He is still athirst for violence and murder. So eager and insatiable is his thirst, that he even breathes out threatening and slaughter (Acts 9:1). His words are spears and arrows, and his tongue a sharp sword. Tis as natural for him to menace the Christians as to breathe the air. Nay, they bled every hour in the purposes of his rancorous heart. It is only owing to want of power that every syllable he utters, every breathe he draws, does not deal out deaths, and cause some of the innocent disciples to fall. Who, upon the principles of human judgment, would not have pronounced him a vessel of wrath, destined to unavoidable damnation? Nay, who would not have been ready to conclude that, if there were heavier chains and a deeper dungeon in the world of woe, they must surely be reserved for such an implacable enemy of true godliness? Yet, admire and adore the inexhaustible treasures of grace-this Saul is admitted into the goodly fellowship of the prophets, is numbered with the noble army of martyrs and makes a distinguished figure among the glorious company of the apostles.

The Corinthians were flagitious even to a proverb. Some of them wallowed in such abominable vices, and habituated themselves to such outrageous acts of injustice, as were a reproach to human nature. Yet even these sons of violence and slaves of sensuality were washed, sanctified, justified (I Cor 6:9-11). "Washed," in the precious blood of a dying Redeemer; "sanctified," by the powerful operations of the blessed Spirit; "justified," through the infinitely tender mercies of a gracious God. Those who were once the burden of the earth are now the joy of heaven, the delight of angels."

The grace of God is so great that the receiver can stretch forth nothing more than hands full of iniquity, and receive in exchange, nothing less than Christ Jesus <u>Himself</u>!

FINDING GRACE IN GOD'S GRAFFITI

※

"And He gave unto Moses, when He had ceased speaking with him upon Mount Sinai, two tables of testimony, tables of stone, written with the finger of God" (Exodus 31:18).

The thoughts of mankind have been recorded since the beginning of time. From the crude etchings upon the stone walls of caves by tribesmen, to the spray painted walls of modern subway stations, man has exposed his heart. The practice of expressing oneself through graffiti transcends cultures and social status. Graffiti is a common method of expression from South America to Northern Ireland, from the Balkans to South Korea.

With His own finger God has written His truth, thereby enabling us to know not only His hand, but also His heart. Beginning with Moses in Exodus 31:18, the laws of God were written with the finger of God upon stone. Why stone? Why not olive tree bark, or better yet, gold or silver? <u>Stone</u> was of God's choosing. "And the tables were the work of God, and the writing was the writing of God..."(Exodus 32:16).

Stone signified permanence. Stone tablets were God's way of confirming that He had made up His mind and would not change. Malahi 3:6 says, "... For I am the Lord, I change not..."

Stone is also hard. Keeping God's laws is hard. In fact, it is the hardest, most difficult activity that you will ever attempt. It is so hard to do that it is impossible to do. The law is demanding, grim, inescapable, and without exception. "For whosoever shall keep the whole law, and yet offend in one point, he is guilty of all" (James 2:10).

Stone is also crushing. My wife and I stood at the base of a mountain in Carracus, Venezuela, where 100,000 people perished in one night during a mud and rock slide. Hugh stones had rushed down the mountainside, crushing both houses and people in their path. In the Old Testament, when an individual violated any one of twenty-six capital offenses, the laws of God were permanent, hard, and crushing, and the penalty of breaking God's laws was death.

God not only wrote in stone (Exodus 31:18), He also wrote in sand. The Gospel of John 8:3-11 tells the story of a woman taken in adultery. The scribes and pharisees were her accusers (verse 3). "They said unto Him, Master, this woman was taken in adultery, in the very act. Now Moses, in the law, commanded us that such should be stoned; but what sayest thou?" (verse 4,5). "...But Jesus stooped down, and with His finger wrote on the ground...So when they continued asking Him, He lifted Himself up, and said unto them, He that is without sin among you, let him first cast a stone at her. And again He stooped down, and wrote on the ground" (verses 6-7).

Now the same finger that wrote in the stone writes in the sand. What is sand? Crushed stone! Jesus wrote in the sand twice. No one knows for sure what he wrote, but He may have written the names Tamar, Rahab, and Bathsheba. Tamar, a adulterous woman, conceived twin sons with her father-in-law. Rahab was the harlot of Jericho. Bathsheba, was the woman for whom King David committed murder and adultery. All three women are found in the lineage of Jesus (Matthew 1).

Jesus was the woman's Rock of Salvation (Psalms 89:26), A Rock "...stricken, smitten of God... wounded for our transgressions...bruised for our iniquities...(Isaiah 53:4,5). The law that was written in crushing stone, was now being fulfilled in the Rock that was to be crushed. Jesus would bear upon Himself her sin...your sin.

There is one more place God wrote His laws… your heart and mind! "This is the covenant that I will make with them after those days, saith the Lord: <u>I will put My laws into their hearts, and in their minds will I write them</u>, and their sins and iniquities will I remember no more" (Hebrews 10:16-17).

What transpired between God writing His law in stone, sand and in your heart, was the cross. So complete was the work of the cross, that the very law that defined righteousness is written in the heart of every believer. Your Father has reconciled you to Himself by Jesus Christ (2 Corinthians 5:18). The exchange has occurred. Jesus was made to be sin for you, so that you might be made the righteousness of God in Christ! (2 Corinthians 5:21).

God's graffiti in stone is truth. God's graffiti in sand is grace. God's graffiti in your heart and mind is glory!

"Allow the greatest of His love to engulf you. Don't resist it. Let the finite experiences of your life be swallowed up by infinite love. Take your eyes off your circumstances. Look at Him. Stop worrying about tomorrow. Look at Him. Turn away from regrets about the past. Look at Him. Whatever distracts you, disturbs you, dilutes you…turn away from it all and look at Him."

Steve McVey
Grace Walk Ministries

FINDING GRACE IN THE EYES OF GOD

☙

"But Noah found grace in the eyes of the Lord" (Genesis 6:8).

There is one statement in the entirety of the Scripture that sets Noah apart from condemned mankind, of whom the Lord said, "…I will destroy…" (Genesis 6:7). "But Noah found grace in the eyes of the Lord." Like every individual that has received the gift of eternal life through Christ Jesus, it was by grace that Noah was saved, through faith, and that not of himself. His salvation was not of himself. His faith was not of himself.

Grace will be found only <u>of</u> the Lord, and <u>in</u> the Lord. It will only be received <u>from</u> the Lord.

You may seek the favor of man. You may strive to win their favor. The favor of man is a strong allurement. It will preserve your reputation. It will eliminate the need to deny yourself. It will eliminate the possibility of suffering for <u>Christ's</u> sake. But, you will, most assuredly, suffer for <u>your own</u> sake as did the people in the day of Noah. Ultimately, if you seek favor in the eyes of man, man can only give unto you what man possesses. Genesis 6 tells us mankind received God's judgment. Man has only that to offer you. But grace will only be found in the eyes of the Lord.

Not only were God's eyes the eyes of grace, they were also the eyes of judgment. Both mercy and justice resided at the same source…the Lord. The same eyes that extended grace to Noah (Genesis 6:8) <u>saw</u> that the wickedness of man was great in the earth (6:5), and <u>saw</u> corruption everywhere as He looked upon the earth (6:12). The sinful world that surrounded Noah found judgment in the eyes of the Lord, and received it.

But Noah found favor in the eyes of God. He received the grace that only God could offer. Genesis 8:1 says, "And God remembered Noah…" Noah and his household were saved from judgment, and were instead favored with salvation, protection, and provision for life.

You cannot have both the favor of God and man. In whose eyes will you find favor? Grace will only be found in the eyes of the Lord.

SHARING THE SAME OPINION WITHOUT CONDEMNATION

☬

"Let this mind be in you, which was also in Christ Jesus" (Philippians 2:5).

It is God's intent that you have the same opinion as Jesus regarding all issues. If you and Jesus view things differently, He is right. Your spirit has been redeemed and delivered from eternal damnation. Yet your mind continually wages war against guilt and condemnation. The forces of darkness have one major assignment as regards believers...to convince you to think differently than Jesus.

God has made certain that you will know what Jesus is thinking. He has written it in your mind! "...I will put my laws into their hearts, and in their minds will I write them" (Hebrews 10:16). This is good news. Paul said, "For I delight in the law of God after the inward man" (Romans 7:22).

God writing His laws in your mind doesn't eliminate conflict, but elevates truth. This holy transaction enables you to have the mind of Christ with certainty. The conflict is real. Paul confessed that "...I see another law in my members. Oh, wretched man that I am! Who shall deliver me from this body of death? I thank God through Jesus Christ, our Lord. So, then, with the mind I myself serve the law of God, but with the flesh, the law of sin" (Romans 8:1).

Your deliverance from condemnation is the mind of Christ. The life of Christ in you enables you to view things as Christ does. You have His spiritual judgment for all things without the condemnation of being judged by any man. "But he that is spiritual judgeth all things, yet he himself is judged of no man. For who hath known the mind of the Lord, that he may instruct him? But we have the mind of Christ" (I Corinthians 2:15-16). You have the mind of Christ! To believe otherwise is to have an opinion different than Christ. HE IS RIGHT!

GOD'S WILL AND OUR OPTIONS

♕

> "...for this is the will of God in Christ Jesus concerning you" (I Thessalonians 5:18)

The will of God is being done in the earth. Jesus prayed to the Father, "Thy will be done in earth, as it is in heaven", (Matthew 6:10). Jesus never prayed a prayer the Father did not hear, and answer.

Now we as believers have two options. We shall either <u>submit</u> to the will of God, or we shall <u>delight</u> in the will of God. The Son of God departed heaven not merely as an act of submission to the will of His Father, but delighting in the will of His Father.

What you believe about yourself ultimately determines <u>how</u> you respond to the will of God. Do you believe you are a servant of God or a son of God? If you believe you are a servant, you will believe that you have primarily been "saved to serve" God and you will <u>submit</u> to his will. You will <u>submit</u> not because you desire to, but because you <u>have</u> to. Servants submit to the will of the <u>Master</u> so they can receive the wage they <u>earned</u>. Submission is a requirement to "stay in good" with the Master. Servants think submission is their only option. But it is not.

Scripture suggests that your high, holy, and heavenly calling is <u>sonship</u> not servanthood. Jesus, the Son, enjoyed this option. He <u>delighted</u> to do the will of the Father. He cooperated enthusiastically.

Jesus trusted the Father and delighted to do His will even though it meant His own death. Jesus said, "For I came down from heaven, not to do mine own will but the will of Him that sent me (John 6:38). <u>Jesus the Son served His Father with delight</u>.

You, too, are a son. "Beloved now are we the sons of God…" (I John 3:2). Sons will serve the Father, but with an entirely different motivation than a servant. Sons <u>delight</u> in the will of the Father. Sons <u>delight</u> because, as a son, what you inherit is not what you deserve or earn. What a son receives is based upon the performance of the Father. Unlike a servant who obtains by achieving, sons acquire by receiving.

If you desire to view your highest calling from God as a call to serve Him, get in line. The heavens are full of angels that serve God at His beckoned call.

On the other hand, should you choose to believe that your highest calling is sonship, get prepared to receive more than you have ever imagined from a Father Who has more than you could ever earn. As a son, trusting your Father will cause you to <u>delight</u> in whatever His will is for you, as it was for Jesus, the Son. You will proclaim, with Him, to your Father, "I <u>delight</u> to do Thy will, O God…"

SONSHIP GONE SOUR

Luke 15:28-29 "And he was angry, and would not go in; therefore came his father out, and entreated him. And he, answering, said to his father, Lo these many years do I serve thee, neither transgressed I at any time thy commandment; and yet thou never gavest me a kid, that I might make merry with my friends."

The prodigal son had returned home, wanting nothing more than to be a servant to his father (Luke 15:19). It was within the father's authority and power to grant him his request for servanthood. Prodded by an ample supply of guilt, and relief to be home from the hog pens, this prodigal son would have made an excellent servant for sure.

His request was founded on his unworthiness. He evaluated his sonship by the level of his performance as a son. At what point in time did the prodigal son cease to be a prodigal?

The older son insisted on having his worthiness celebrated. He desired, more than anything, to be recognized for his great service to his father, and for the fact that while rendering such great service, he never transgressed any rule or regulation at any time. He believed that his sonship was based on being a faithful servant. At what point in time did the older son become the prodigal?

Notice the father initiates contact with both sons right where they are (Luke 15:20,28). The father comes to them. Neither worthiness nor unworthiness qualified them as sons.

Prodigal sonship is the result of evaluating your relationship with the Father based on your efforts, good or bad, not His. Sleeping in the hog pens of life will convince you that only mountains of good deeds will insure sonship, and cause you to be accepted back into the family of God. Keeping all the rules will produce the greater deception. The better you believe you're doing at obeying the rules, the more convinced you will be that the Father is pleased because of it. Both views are evidence of a prodigal on the loose.

For all sons full of condemnation or pride, the Father is constantly coming to you where you are. Agree with Him. Accept His evaluation of you as His son. Receive His invitation. Enjoy the Party.

THE EVER CHANGING METHOD OF A NEVER CHANGING GOD

Malachi 3:6 says, "For I am Lord, I change not…" Hebrews 13:8 speaks of "Jesus Christ, the same yesterday, and today, and forever." Regarding the Lord, James 1:17 says, "…with whom is no variableness, neither shadow of turning." In other words, the Lord God has made up His mind, and that settles it! His Word is settled and true, His heart is steadfast, and both His love and judgments are sure.

It is common for the focus of man to be upon the procedures of God, and not the Person of God. We want very much to know and see what God is doing, but desire less to know Him and Him alone. If you settle for knowing only the methods, procedures, or hand of God, you have not sought to know God. The Lord is ever changing His methods. A primary purpose for varying His manner of working in your life is to provoke you to know Him.

The same God that gave victory to Joshua at mighty Jericho gave Joshua victory in diminutive, and seemingly insignificant Ai. Both cities were gifts from God to Israel. Jericho was given to Joshua (Joshua 6:2), and Ai was given into the hand of Joshua (Joshua 8:1). The same God gave victory, but by completely different methods.

To receive the victory that God had given Israel at Jericho, trumpets sounded, the people shouted, and "…the wall fell flat…" (Joshua 6:20). After a resounding defeat at the tiny village of Ai,

God gave Ai to Israel His way. Ambush and surprise became God's methods of choice.

If on your journey you stop and enshrine one of God's methods that was particularly meaningful to you at a certain juncture in your life, you will ultimately worship His procedure instead of Him. You will soon conclude that the Lord cannot work in any other manner. Soon you will judge another's testimony of God's work as unsound, because it is unlike your experience, and thus, unlike God.

Jesus healed many people that were blind. But rarely was His method identical. Why? Because the emphasis was on the Healer, not healing.

<u>The never changing God, utilizes ever changing methods</u>. You must know that <u>in the workings of God, the "Who" is vastly more important than the "how"</u>. Proverbs 3:6 tells us that, "In all thy ways acknowledge Him, and He shall direct thy paths." We have given glory to God's methods, but He will never share His glory, even with His own methodology. When we give glory to his methods, we fail to give glory to Him. You cannot do both.

When the church is divided over God's methods, we are doing something the Lord never ordained. He never made His methods the focus. He is our focus.

<u>God may change the method by which He receives glory, but He will never change the fact that all glory belongs to Him and Him alone</u>.

"Jesus is enough. Church will only carry you so far, but Jesus is enough. Dedication and rededication will fail you, but Jesus is enough. Good intentions will abandon you, but Jesus is enough. Trying harder is no answer at all, but Jesus is enough".

Steve McVey
Grace Walk Ministries

HIMSELF ALONE

❦

"Oh, the depth of the riches both of the wisdom and knowledge of God! How unsearchable are His judgements, and His ways past finding out!" (Romans 11:33)

"For of Him, and through Him, and to Him, are all things: to whom be glory forever. Amen. (Romans 11:36)

You do not live <u>for</u> God. You live <u>from</u> God. There is no life apart from Him. The strength of a man's standing with God is not measured by what the man does for God. It is always measured by <u>what the Lord is doing for the man</u>. As a new creation in Christ (II Cor. 5:17), life is defined by dependency, not discipline; by relationship, not regulations and rules; by desire, not duty; by a person, a promise, not personal performance; by trusting, not trying.

Himself
By: A.B. Simpson

Once it was the blessing, Now it is the Lord;
Once it was the feeling, Now it is His word;
Once His gift I wanted, Now the Giver own;
Once I sought for healing, Now Himself alone.

Once 'twas painful trying, Now 'tis perfect trust;
Once a half salvation, Now the uttermost;
Once 'twas ceaseless holding, Now he holds me fast;
Once 'twas constant drifting, Now my anchor's cast.

Once 'twas busy planning, Now 'tis trustful prayer;
Once 'twas anxious caring, Now He has the care;
Once 'twas what I wanted, Now what Jesus says;
Once 'twas constant asking, Now 'tis ceaseless praise.

Once it was working, His it hence shall be;
Once I tried to use Him, Now He uses me;
Once the power I wanted, Now the Mighty one;
Once for self I labored, Now for Him alone.

Once I hoped in Jesus, Now I know He's mine;
Once my lamps were dying, Now they brightly shine;
Once for death I waited, Now His coming hail;
And my hopes are anchored, Safe within the veil.

CHORUS: All in all forever,
 Jesus will I sing,
 Everything in Jesus,
 And Jesus everything.

Your life is not about you. It is ALL about Jesus Himself…and Himself alone. To His children, God never gives you less than Himself!

To contact the author please write to:

John A. Knox
P.O. Box 136
Hamilton, GA 31811